Moon Astral Talisman.
Flawless moonstone
handcrafted in 21k gold.
Piece no.859

Aum 'Om' Pendant. Flawless
diopside handcrafted in
21k gold. Piece no.93

Auspicious Invocation

"My Lord, You are unlimited. Even the predominating deities of the higher planetary systems, including Lord *Brahma,* could not find Your limitations. Nor could You Yourself ascertain the limit of Your qualities. Like atoms in the sky, there are multi-universes, and these are rotating in due course of time. All the experts in *Vedic* understanding are searching for You by eliminating the material elements. In this way, searching and searching, they come to the conclusion that everything is complete in You. Thus You are the resort of everything. This is the conclusion of all *Vedic* experts."

Srimad-Bhagavata Maha-puranam: 10.87.41

Translation by His Divine Grace
Srila A.C. Bhaktivedanta Swami Prabhupada

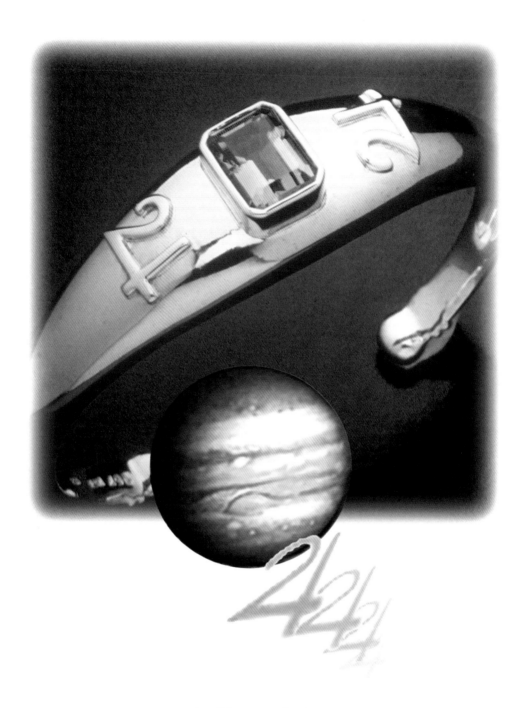

A striking example of a
Jupiter Astral Talisman.
Flawless citrine handcrafted
in silver and 18k gold.
Piece no.167

ANCIENT ASTROLOGICAL GEMSTONES & TALISMANS

The Complete Science of Planetary Gemology

Compiled in Asia 1968 – 1994 by *Richard S. Brown* Gemologist (G.I.A.)

ANCIENT ASTROLOGICAL GEMSTONES & TALISMANS

Author:
Richard S. Brown, Jr.

Editor:
Dan Reid

Art Editor:
Manfred Winkler

Photography:
Adisorn Wattanavanich

Editorial Contributors
and Advisors:
Tom Hopke
Pandit Vidyadhar Shukla

ISBN:
974-89022-4-2

Publishers:
A.G.T. Co. Ltd.
99/22 Soi 7, Lang Suan Road,
Pathumwan, Bangkok 10330
Thailand

Design, Typography,
Image manipulation:
Asea Aerolights Co. Ltd.
Omni Solutions Co. Ltd.

Pre-Press:
Omni Solutions Co. Ltd.
Asea Aerolights Co. Ltd.

Printers:
Thai Watana Panich Press Co. Ltd.

Rahu and Ketu Astral Talisman.
Flawless spessartine and cat's eyes
with onyx handcrafted in 21k
gold. Piece no.2

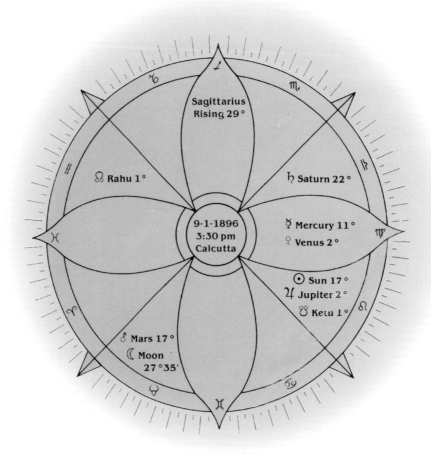

Sagittarius
Rising 29°

☊ Rahu 1°

♄ Saturn 22°

9-1-1896
3:30 pm
Calcutta

☿ Mercury 11°
♀ Venus 2°

☉ Sun 17°
♃ Jupiter 2°
☋ Ketu 1°

♂ Mars 17°
☽ Moon
27°35'

Astrological chart of His Divine Grace Srila A. C. Bhaktivedanta Swami Prabhupada, who obtained and still is wearing a blue sapphire for its powerful Saturn influence, as advised by his personal Jyotishacarya (astrologer) in Sridham Vrindavan.

◆ ————————————————

Chart cast by *Nalini-kanta Dasa*

A Dedication

I dedicate this book to His Divine Grace
Srila A.C. Bhaktivedanta Swami Prabhupada,
my Gurudeva,
who opened the flood-gates of *Vedic* wisdom in this
age of darkness.

My thanks are due to Dan Reid for editing this book
and also to Tom Hopke and *Pandit Vidyadhar Shukla*
for contributing important astrological insights.

Ketu Astral Talisman.
Flawless cat's eyes and
yellow beryl with sacred
herbs handcrafted in
21k gold. Piece no.450

Table of Contents

Nava-Ratna.
The nine planetary
gems handcrafted in
21k gold.
Piece no.27

Introduction

According to ancient *Vedic* authority, natural gemstones transmit astral powers like radio crystals transform sound! Fine, flawless gems promote good fortune, while poor quality gems have the opposite effect (ref. ***Garuda Purana:*** chapter 68, verse 17). The power of gems emanates from the nine planets (*nava-graha*) recognized by the Asian, 'Sidereal' science of astrology. The nine planets and their associated gems are ruby for the Sun, pearl for the Moon, yellow sapphire for Jupiter, hessonite for *Rahu* (the ascending node of the Moon), emerald for Mercury, diamond for Venus, cat's eye for *Ketu* (the descending node of the Moon), blue sapphire for Saturn and coral for Mars (ref. ***Mani Mala:*** page 575, verse 79). These 'planets' influence different aspects of life and, as luminous bodies, also radiate specific cosmic colors. According to ancient belief the colors radiated by the nine planets are identical to the cosmic colors of the different gemstones. Sometimes the cosmic colors are obvious while in other cases this is not so. Thus red is the cosmic color of rubies, while orange is the cosmic color of pearls.

Gemstones strengthen planetary powers and will boost their specific influences in three ways. The first way is by adding 'cosmic color' to one's own aura. The second way is by 'astrologically' enhancing their associated area of one's life. For instance, Moon (pearl) influences mind and emotions while Venus (diamond) rules art and sex. The third way is by attracting the attention of their ruling planetary deities, the Sun-god, Moon-god, Mars, Jupiter, etc. The 'cosmic colors' and gemstone powers will be explained further in chapter III.

There are five basic methods for choosing gemstones: The first is determined by one's birth '*rasi*' or zodiac (Moon) sign. Thus the sign of Leo is ruled by the Sun and the planetary gemstone is ruby (or any fine red gemstone like red spinel or red garnet). The second method is based on one's birth constellation or '*naksatra*'. Everyone is born under one of the 27 constellations and each constellation is ruled by one of the nine planets. Thus the ruling planet's gemstone is recognized as one's 'birth star gem'. The third choice is based on one's *Lagna* or 'rising sign'. In a horoscope with Leo rising, Leo is ruled by the Sun, so the 'rising sign gem' would be ruby or another Sun jewel. The forth way to choose one's planetary gem is based on preference. If a person is attracted to the influence of a particular stone, and provided it isn't a 'dangerous' planetary gem (*krura-graha-ratna*) or a harmful influence in their horoscope (i.e. located in a debilitated rasi, an enemy rasi, or other evil position) then one can use the gem of one's liking. (**Note:** This last point should also be bourn in mind when choosing gems for *rasi, naksatra* or *lagna*). The fifth and most specific method is based on the prescription of a qualified 'Sidereal' astrologer. The astrologer casts a person's horoscope and studies the position of the nine planets at the time of one's birth to determine which planet(s) would be most beneficial to 'strengthen'. Time periods for using certain gemstones may also be prescribed based on one's *Mahadasha* or 'major planetary periods', *Antardasha* or 'sub-periods', as well as other deeper astrological considerations. This last method is the most potent way to choose gemstones for their powers. It is very important to consult with an expert **Sidereal** astrologer. More detailed information on this subject is found in chapter VI. *Vedic* knowledge concerning gemstone 'clarity' or purity, and esoteric information on preparing 'Astral Gemstone Talismans' may be found in chapters IV and V respectively.

The single biggest obstacle to the world-wide, modern day practice of 'Planetary Gemology' is wide-spread acceptance of the so-called birth stone system from the West. The history of this practice is explained in chapter II. It is no secret that this list of birth stones was created by the American National Retail Jewelers' Association in 1912. The origin of this system is attributed to early Hebrew civilization and has nothing what-so-ever to do with **any** system of astrology. Furthermore, birth stones cannot be based on a list of months because birth signs change on or about the 22nd of each month. Thus two different signs rule each month according to the date of one's birth.

The color hue of each gem will almost always fit into one of the four social-economic-intellectual categories (*varnas*). Everyone is advised to use the color that best suits their needs. Refer to chapter III for this information.

Ancient Astrological Gemstones & Talismans combines the essential knowledge from the ancient Vedic texts with modern gemological data. We sincerely hope that readers find the resulting information both helpful and enlightening.

It is our hope and belief that this ancient knowledge of 'Planetary Gemology' we are representing will soon become an important part of World culture and will be remembered and practiced for at least 1,000 years into the future.

Venus Astral Talisman.
Flawless white sapphire
handcrafted in
21k gold Piece no.106

– Richard S. Brown
(Hrisikesananda dasa)

(Bangkok, Jan. 2nd, 1994)

Author's Note:

Ignorant Skepticism vs Time-Honored Wisdom

Planetary Gemology:
The sidereal astrological science of the relationship
between gemstones and the nine planets.

IN 1987 I was invited by the President of the Asian Institute of Gemological Sciences (AIGS) to give a lecture to his students on the subject of 'Planetary Gemology'. The audience was extremely interested in the discourse when suddenly I was interrupted by a student who insisted that everything I had said was total nonsense. My question to all sane and level-headed persons is how do you qualify to pass judgement on any subject? How do scientists and philosophers arrive at any conclusion? The student had done no conclusive research nor testing, yet still had the audacity to pass a completely unqualified judgement!

For thousands of years great thinkers and scientists such as *Vyasadeva* (the compiler of the *Vedas*), *Sri Parasara Rishi* (A grand-guru of sidereal astrology), *Sri Bhakti-siddhanta Sarasvati* (a great *Vedic* scholar and *Vaisnava* leader), and *Pandit Vidyadhar Shukla* (a leading astrologer and the Chief Brahmin Priest of Thailand) have revered and practiced the ancient *Vedic* science of *Jyotish* or sidereal astrology. And for that matter, millions of intelligent people today still believe in and follow this ancient science. Who are we, puny, uncontrolled and unqualified humans, to call all these, and other learned persons fools?! Who is thus qualified?

Certainly there is a criteria for making a judgement. This criteria is, and always will be, **knowledge!** Without knowledge of a subject, no one is qualified to pass judgement with any certainty. Especially when dealing with subjects far surpassing our limited sensual or intellectual experiences. Consider this: how many people today have stopped to think that this solid Earth we stand upon is actually a planet which is flying through space at break-neck speed? And this earth is not alone! Look to the heavens on any clear night and behold the breathtaking array and multitude of other planets and stars reaching far beyond even the most powerful telescopes. The planets in our own solar system are also curving through space at varying speeds in orbits around a Sun; and all these heavenly bodies (including this Earth we live on) are moving through space like the workings of a great, cosmic clock. This has been going on since the beginning of time, in spite of the ignorance and limited knowledge of humans, animals, and others. In the face of this vast and wonderful material reality, who is qualified to understand or pass judgement on the ancient sciences of sidereal astrology and planetary gemology. One look at the great personalities who have properly accepted and investigated *Vedic* wisdom since time immemorial will answer my question. Both past as well as present, these great teachers obtained and revered the **time-honored wisdom**. Others, though completely un-versed in certain fields or branches of knowledge, but who still speak against them are undoubtedly **ignorant skeptics!** Without undertaking a well-rounded course of research no one is qualified to reject anything, especially ancient, time-honored wisdom, out of hand. Both science and logic dictate wisdom based on divine revelation combined with extensive experimentation and first-hand experience. The peoples of Asia since time immemorial are certainly **not** fools. In our quest for life we must not lose sight of the greater realities.

**Remember, we are living on a small planet which is
gravitating through space at this very moment.**

◆————————

3

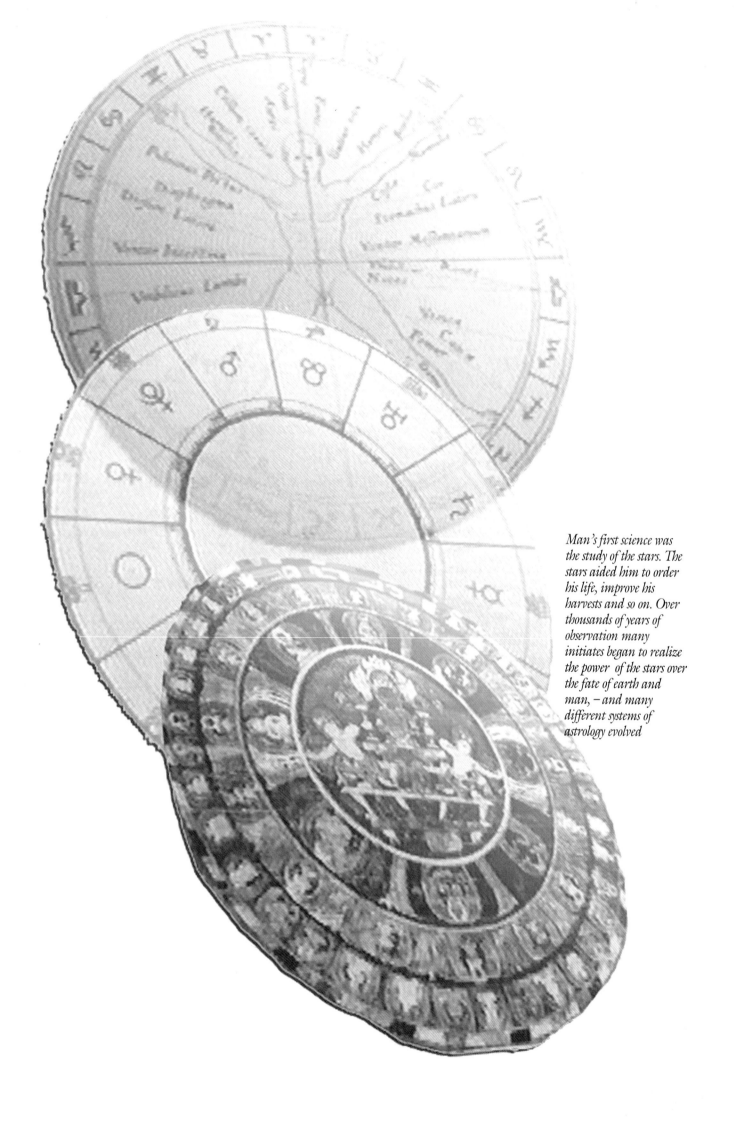

Man's first science was
the study of the stars. The
stars aided him to order
his life, improve his
harvests and so on. Over
thousands of years of
observation many
initiates began to realize
the power of the stars over
the fate of earth and
man, – and many
different systems of
astrology evolved

I
Sidereal Astrology

"Learned astrologers can indicate what may take place in the future. Only the Creator can say what will definitely happen."

The Astrological Magazine, Sept. 1992, p.673

THE use of planetary gem therapy described in this book is based upon the Eastern or **Sidereal** system of astrology. Therefore, it is important that the reader first understand this ancient science and realize how it differs from the modern 'Tropical' system.

The practice of '*Jyotish*' or Sidereal astrology has been in continuous use in India for thousands of years and in recent years has become increasingly popular in the West as well. This method gives clear indications about one's personality and personal proclivities, and also uses predictive methods which are useful for short or long range planning in one's life. The study of the twelve houses of the Sidereal horoscope reveals one's destiny in all areas of life. For example, the first house and the Sun in one's chart will indicate the health of the person. The second house and Jupiter reveal one's karmic destiny in the area of finances. Similarly, Saturn and Mercury represent one's profession and business, the ninth house represents religious pursuits, and there are even formulas for understanding the past and future lives of the soul.

The Sidereal or Eastern system of astrology is based on the position of the belt of fixed stars and constellations in the heavens, whereas the Tropical zodiac or the Western astrological system is based upon the position of the Sun in relation to the Earth. The first degree of the Sidereal zodiac is measured from a point 180° opposite the star Spica, whereas the first degree of the Western zodiac occurs when the Sun reaches the position above the equator known as the vernal equinox, on or about the 22nd of March each year.

Originally, the first degree of the zodiac was common to both systems. Due to the peculiarities in the Earth's orbit, however, the belt of stars and constellations appears to shift in relation to the Tropical zodiac. As a result, the two zodiacs are drifting apart. This is called the 'procession of the equinoxes', and today the difference between the two systems is calculated at about 23°. Thus, if a person is born on January 1, he will have the Sun in Capricorn according to the Western system, but according to the Sidereal system the Sun will be at approximately 16° Sagittarius.

By practical experience, and in light of the advice of the great sages of India, the use of the Sidereal method is preferable. It is mathematically more correct, and it also penetrates into the subtle elements of nature, such as mind, intellect, and spirit to present a more complete picture of our soul's sojourn in the realm of time and space.

The Sidereal astrological system notes the strengths and weaknesses that a person will experience in life, and also recommends remedial measures for improving our future. The *karma* or destiny we are born with has been accrued by pious and impious activities in previous births. The spiritual astrology of India opines that *karma* is not eternal and can be changed. There are several ways to strengthen our planetary *karma*.

The easiest method is to wear gemstones which attract the pure vibrations of the planets. According to a person's birth chart gems can be recommended to counteract negative influences, strengthen auspicious planets, or, according to a person's particular desire, a gem may be worn to help fulfill a certain ambition. A good astrologer should be consulted for particulars.

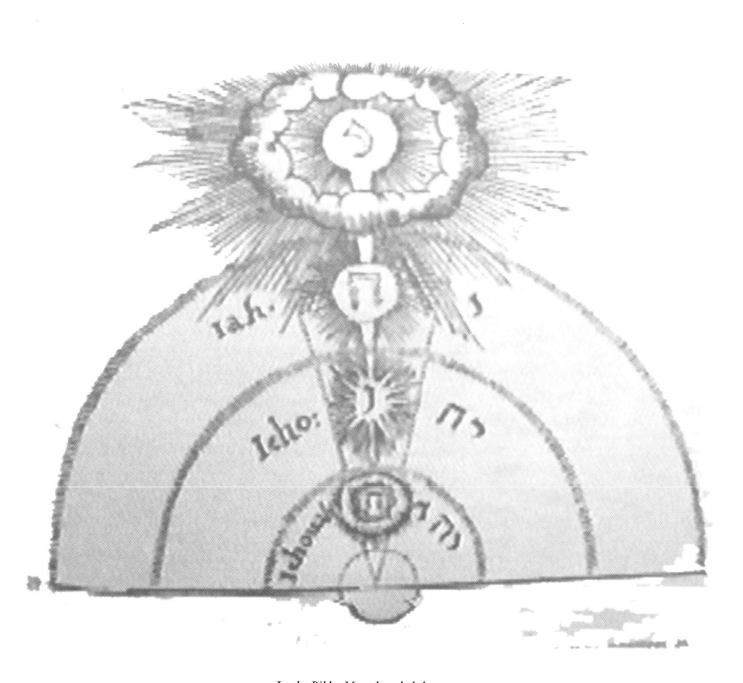

In the Bible, Moses handed down
rules governing the Breastplate of Judgment
which contained 12 gems, each engraved with the
name of one of the twelve tribes of Israel. Another
arrangement of the 12 gems is described in the
Book of Revelation as the foundation stones
of the New Jerusalem. The order in which
these 12 gems were given was used by the American
National Retail Jewelers' Association to determine
the succession of birthstones for the months.
**Obviously this currently recognized
Western Birthstone System has nothing to do
with any astrological science.**

II
Birth Stones

According to the Gemological Institute of America (ref. G.I.A. Colored Stones Course, assignment #41, 'Birthstones'), the origin of the Western system of birthstones can be traced to the Breastplate of the High Priest. In the Bible, Moses handed down rules governing the Breastplate of Judgment which contained 12 gems, each engraved with the name of one of the twelve tribes of Israel. Another arrangement of the 12 gems is described in the Book of Revelation as the foundation stones of the New Jerusalem. The order in which these 12 gems were given was used to determine the succession of birthstones for the months.

On August 12, 1912 the American National Retail Jewelers' Association arbitrarily substituted a new list of birthstones, adding to or changing many of the traditional stones to others which were more commercially viable. In 1938 the American Gem Society adopted this list (with the addition of citrine) for use by its members. In 1952 a variation of this list was approved by the American National Retail Jewelers Association (ANRJA), National Jewelers Association (NJA), and the American Gem Society (AGS). Thus the official list of Western birthstones was established as follows:

MONTH	BIRTHSTONE
January	Garnet
February	Amethyst
March	Bloodstone or Aquamarine
April	Diamond
May	Emerald
June	Pearl or Moonstone (also Alexandrite)
July	Ruby
August	Sardonyx or Peridot
September	Sapphire
October	Opal or Pink Tourmaline
November	Topaz or Citrine
December	Turquoise or Zircon

In light of the above, it is obvious that the currently recognized Western Birthstone System has **nothing to do with any astrological science**. It should also be noted that the signs of the zodiac change on or about the 22nd of each month. Therefore it is impossible to establish a list of birthstones based on the months. According to the Tropical System of astrology prevalent in the West, zodiac or birth signs are determined by the position of the Sun in one's horoscope. In the Sidereal system this is determined by the position of the Moon. But in both systems, the zodiac sign is important, not the month of one's birth. Each sign of the zodiac (*rasi*) is ruled by one of the planets and each planet in turn rules over certain gemstones according to their color. In Asia these birthstones are known collectively as **Nava-Ratna** or the nine (astral) gems.

*Nava-Ratna. The nine
planetary gems handcrafted
in 21k gold. Piece no.23*

The only logical system of birthstones is based upon the planet ruling one's zodiac sign.

The following list of **birthstones** is known and accepted throughout Asia since ancient times:

BIRTHSTONE	RULING PLANET	ZODIAC SIGN
Ruby	Sun	Leo
Pearl	Moon	Cancer
Coral	Mars	Aries, Scorpio
Emerald	Mercury	Gemini, Virgo
Yellow Sapphire	Jupiter	Sagittarius, Pisces
Diamond	Venus	Taurus, Libra
Blue Sapphire	Saturn	Capricorn, Aquarius
Hessonite	*Rahu*	*
Cat's eye	*Ketu*	*

* According to *B.V. Raman* and other authorities, since *Rahu* and *Ketu* are *aprakasha* or shadowy planets, they will reflect the qualities of the lord of the (zodiac) sign they are in. If *Rahu* is located in Leo, a sign ruled by the Sun, look to the position of Sun in the chart and expect similar effects for *Rahu*. **Note:** Other natural stones can be substituted according to color. These secondary choice gems are known collectively as '*Upa-Ratna*' or alternate stones. These secondary choice jewels are listed in chapters III and IV.

The most important difference in the use of astrological gems by the two systems is that in the Eastern system gems are recognized as possessing unique planetary powers which may be prescribed for specific purposes. We must first look to see which planets (if any) are in their 'own sign' (sign ownership), or are 'exalted' (maximum strength) or in '*mulatrikona*' (trine), or at least in a 'friendly sign'. All of these 'auspicious' planetary sign positions give positive results and will be beneficial to 'strengthen'. Wearing gems to 'pacify' afflicted planets has not proven beneficial in our experience. Planets which are in a harmful condition in one's horoscope should not be made stronger, except when under the watchful eye of a 'selfless' Sidereal astrologer.

In the next chapter we will discuss the 'powers' of fine gemstones, planet by planet.

Ancient Indian Stone carvings of the 'Two Faces of the Moon', symbolising the radiating powers of Rahu and Ketu

Saturn Astral
Talisman. Flawless,
unburned blue
sapphire handcrafted
in 18k gold.
Piece no.179

III
Gemstone Powers

THE astrological powers of gemstones are derived from the special cosmic influences of their associated ruling planets. The term 'planet' used in Sidereal astrology refers to a celestial body or 'point' which has the property of attraction. Hence the Sun (a star), the Moon (a satellite of the Earth), and *Rahu* and *Ketu* (two points of concourse of orbits of the Earth and the Moon) are referred to under the somewhat forced name of 'planet'. Uranus, Neptune, Pluto, and a host of others are considered to have no effect on human affairs. These move in the heavens with ranging velocities influenced by other forces. (ref. **Astrology For Beginners** by *B.V. Raman*, chapter I, page 5). Prof. *B. Suryanarain Rao* states that "Men are continuously subjected to the influences of planetary rays." These planetary rays are radiated as gravitational, electrical and magnetic energy fields which are transmitted as light waves. These light waves can be measured from their smallest part as fractional parts of a billionth of an inch, to ones which are billions of billions of miles in length. Each of the nine planets (*nava-graha*) influences us according to it's nature. Therefore, a knowledge of these planetary influences is essential to any understanding of gemstones and their powers.

The gemological texts of India explain that white light is actually composed of seven primary and two secondary colors blended together. The seven colors are red, orange, yellow, green, blue, indigo and violet; the other two colors are ultra-violet and infra-red. The seven primary colors become visible in the form of a rainbow whenever white light is defracted through a prism or rain drops; but the two secondary colors always remain invisible.

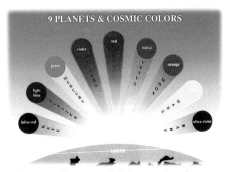

The nine planets and their cosmic colors

These nine colors are understood to be the cosmic matrix and very essence of the nine planets; and it is through these colors that the planets radiate their energy and influence. When the visible colored-light waves are measured, infra-red exhibits the longest wave length and ultra-violet, the shortest. It is important to note that the wave length of colored-light emanating from the nine planets is believed to match those radiating from each planet's corresponding gemstone(s). For example, the wave-length of light emanating from the Sun is identical to that exhibited by a ruby – both are red.

*Sun and Jupiter Astral
Talisman. Flawless
Burmese red spinel and
matching yellow sapphires
handcrafted in 18k gold.
Piece no.300*

Among all the elements in nature, gemstones constitute the most condensed form of concentrated color. Gems provide an inexhaustible source of cosmic color rays. These planetary gemstone colors are described in this chapter under their ruling planet.

The following is a list of the special influences exerted on human affairs by each of the nine planets along with the particular powers ascribed to their corresponding gemstones.

1. Sun (Surya)

The Sun is the sovereign planet of the zodiac, furnishing the light and heat upon which all life depends. The Sun's position in a person's horoscope determines his or her external appearance and public persona and provides the energy for one's personal power and influence over others. The Sun governs the fields of philosophy, government service, churches and temples, the medical profession, gold trade and public fame. Solar energy is associated with the fire element, the color red, fatherhood and masculinity, royalty and political power.

If the Sun is exalted one will be well-read, pious, strong, compassionate and untroubled. But if the position of the Sun in one's horoscope is weak or afflicted then contrary results may be expected. **Red** is the cosmic color transmitted by rubies and other natural red gems. Red color waves are hot and therefore useful in curing diseases caused by excessive cold and moisture in the body, viz. cold, flu, anemia, low blood pressure, heart and circulatory problems, as well as foolish behavior and learning deficiencies. In addition, Solar gemstones confer courage, eliminate sadness, moderate excess sensuality, and help elevate one's status in society.

Gemstones ruled by the Sun are natural ruby, red spinel, red garnet, rubellite and other natural pink or red gems with crystal clear transparency. In order to properly transmit solar energy, Sun stones must be flawless (eye-clean) and should be set in gold.

Note: As the Sun is incompatible with Saturn, Venus, *Rahu* and *Ketu,* Sun gems such as ruby should not be used with blue sapphire, diamond, hessonite or cat's eye. Specifically designed talismans like the *Nava-Ratna* (nine gems setting) are an exception to this principle.

The particular hue or type of red color recommended for each social-religious-economic station of society are listed as follows:

1) Religious practitioners, scientists and educators should use pink red (most women are also advised to use pink).

2) Soldiers, administrators and bureaucrats should use blood red.

3) Farmers, bankers and traders should use orange red.

4) Servants, laborers and workers should use violet red.

From a rare reproduction of Surya, the Sun god of the Vedic pantheon, here representing the jewels of the Sun

*Moon and Sun Astral
Talisman. Flawless moonstone
and matching red spinels
handcrafted in 18k gold
'herb' ring. Piece no.480*

2. Moon (Chandra)

The Moon governs the mind, and it's position in one's horoscope determines a person's habitual patterns of thought, feeling and volition. It rules all professions associated with water, such as sailing and fishing, and it influences the tidal patterns of oceans and seas as well as bodily fluids. Lunar energy is associated with the water element, the color white, motherhood and femininity, romance and love. The Moon is a soft, sensitive planet with fluid, feminine qualities.

If the Moon is exalted one will be wealthy, industrious and respected. But if the position of the Moon is weak or afflicted then contrary results may be expected. Diabetes, alcohol and drug abuse, and all types of emotional distress are also associated with debilitated Lunar energy. **Orange** is the cosmic color transmitted by pearls and other Lunar gems. Orange color waves are cold and therefore useful in treating diseases of the bodily secretions and blood caused by excessive heat in the body. Fine Moon jewels are known to be helpful in cases of mental derangements caused by an excess of heat in the heart and brain. Moon astral talismans will also enhance all mental faculties, pacify emotions, induce tranquility, and improve artistic creativity.

Gemstones ruled by the Moon are natural pearl & moonstone. Flawless (eye-clean) gems are required in order for Moon astral talismans to properly transmit beneficial Lunar energy.

Note: As the Moon is incompatible with *Rahu* and *Ketu*, Moon gems such as pearl should not be used with hessonite or cat's-eye. Specifically designed talismans like the *Nava-Ratna* (nine gems setting) are an exception to this principle.

The particular hue or type of white color recommended for each social-religious-economic station of society are listed as follows:

1) Religious practitioners, scientists and educators should use white.

2) Soldiers, administrators and bureaucrats should use pinkish to orangish white.

3) Farmers, bankers and traders should use yellow to greenish white.

4) Servants, laborers and workers should use bluish or black.

From a rare reproduction of Chandra, the Moon god of the Vedic pantheon, here representing the jewels of the Moon

Jupiter Astral Talisman.
Flawless citrine handcrafted
in 18k gold. Piece no.340

3. Jupiter (Brihaspati)

Jupiter is the most auspicious and beneficent planet. Wealthy and influential individuals generally possess a strong Jupiter in their horoscopes, and this reflects the rich rewards of positive *karma* accumulated in previous lives. Jupiter governs religious activity, financial affairs, personal happiness, and teaching. Jupiter also determines one's spiritual orientation. It is associated with the color yellow, the bodily fluids, education, pilgrimage places, and transcendental wisdom. The Sanskrit name for Jupiter is *'guru'*, indicating a source of divine knowledge and spiritual insight.

If Jupiter is exalted one will be a leader of men, powerful, respected, although susceptible to anger. But if the position of Jupiter in a person's horoscope is debilitated Jupiter can cause personal unhappiness, egotism, sloth, and legal problems. **Light blue** is the cosmic color transmitted by yellow sapphires and other natural yellow gems. Light blue color waves, being very cold, relate to the ethereal nature and are helpful in curing diseases of the glands, the fat system and bodily cavities. Jupiter astral talismans are known to enhance spiritual understanding, facilitate pregnancy and childbirth, improve marital relations, increase one's fortune, and help balance the endocrine system. Jupiter jewels are known to be especially favorable to women by increasing their happiness and contentment.

Gemstones: Jupiter's energy is transmitted by natural yellow sapphires, topaz, citrine, heliodor, and other flawless (eye-clean) yellow gems.

Note: As Jupiter is incompatible with Mercury and Venus, Jupiter gems such as yellow sapphire should not be used with emerald or diamond. Specifically designed talismans like the *Nava-Ratna* (nine gems setting) are an exception to this principle.

From a rare reproduction of Brihaspati, the god Jupiter , here representing the yellow jewels of Jupiter

The particular hue or type of yellow color recommended for each social-religious-economic station of society are listed as follows:

1) Religious practitioners, scientists and educators should use light yellow.

2) Soldiers, administrators and bureaucrats should use orangy yellow.

3) Farmers, bankers and traders should use golden yellow.

4) Servants, laborers and workers should use greenish yellow.

Rahu Astral Talisman.
Flawless hessonite handcrafted
in 18k gold. Piece no.72

4. Rahu (Moon's North Node)

Rahu is by nature a malevolent planetary influence which can cause personal frustration, sacrileges habits, abuse of alcohol and drugs, possession of ghosts and demons, and infectious diseases. However, when located in a powerful position in one's horoscope, *Rahu* can elevate one to positions of great wealth and power and confer public influence over the masses. *Rahu* is associated with serpents, Buddhism, fear, *karmic* retribution, and un-virtuous characters.

Persons with *Rahu* exalted are wealthy and fortunate. But those with a weak or afflicted *Rahu* in their horoscope have a tendency to suffer from fear of supernatural phenomena and suicidal impulses. **Ultra-Violet** is the cosmic color transmitted by hessonite and other orange gems. Ultra-violet color waves are the coldest of all the cosmic rays and should be used for ailments caused by extreme over-heating, i.e. high fever, hyper-acidity, indigestion, hyper-sexuality, insomnia, and during child birth. *Rahu* astral talismans may also help divert disasters, prevent insanity, counteract poisons, and protect one from demoniac influences. *Rahu* is particularly associated with scientific genius and the ability to deal successfully with people of lower status, such as servants, employees, and underworld characters. In India, it is still common practice to place a fine hessonite gem into the mouth of a deceased person before cremation. This is to insure that the dearly departed will not be obstructed by *Rahu* on their journey through time.

Gemstones governed by *Rahu* include hessonite, spessertite, zircon (hyacinth), and other natural gems of golden-orange to brownish-orange hues. Only flawless (eye-clean) stones transmit beneficial *Rahu* energy.

Note: As *Rahu* is incompatible with Sun and Moon, *Rahu* gems such as hessonite should not be used with ruby or pearl. Specifically designed talismans like the *Nava-Ratna* (nine gems setting) are an exception to this principle.

From a rare Vedic depiction of Rahu, Rising Node of the Moon, here representing the orange jewels of Rahu

The particular hue or type of orange color recommended for each social-religious-economic station of society are listed as follows:

1) Religious practitioners, scientists and educators should use honey orange.

2) Soldiers, administrators and bureaucrats should use red orange.

3) Farmers, bankers and traders should use golden orange.

4) Servants, laborers and workers should use brownish orange.

Mercury Astral Talisman.
Flawless peridot handcrafted
in 21k gold. Piece no.407

5. Mercury (Budha)

Mercury governs intelligence and therefore rules such fields as education, literature, communication, and public speaking. It is associated with the earth element, cold energy, the color green, agriculture, travel, and the nervous system. Endowed with youthful, fast-moving energy, Mercury appears prominently in the horoscopes of people who are playful, enthusiastic, and talkative. Mercury also governs astrologers, clerks, accountants, sculptors, and any other profession requiring skillful use of the hands. Mercury enhances the ability to learn languages, improves memory, and facilitates the power of speech. People with a strong Mercury generally have the ability to perform activities quickly and handle several matters simultaneously.

If Mercury is exalted one will be educated, happy, fortunate and highly respected. But if Mercury occupies a weak or harmful position in one's horoscope, one becomes prone to speech and hearing impediments, deceptive behavior, and lack of vitality. **Green** is the cosmic color transmitted by emeralds and other green gems. Green color waves relate to the earth element and are cold by nature. This color, being heavy, influences the heavy organs of the body such as the flesh, liver, kidneys and intestines. Mercury astral talismans are also known to enhance psychic powers, improve memory and learning, strengthen the nervous system, and provide protection against snakes and envious people.

Gemstones governed by Mercury include emerald, peridot, tsavorite, tourmaline, diopside, green jade and other natural green gems of flawless (eye-clean) quality.

Note: As Mercury is incompatible with Mars and Jupiter, Mercury gems such as emerald should not be used with coral or yellow sapphire. Specifically designed talismans like the *Nava-Ratna* (nine gems setting) are an exception to this principle.

From a rare depiction of Budha, the Vedic deity of Mercury; here representing the green jewels of Budha

The particular hue or type of green color recommended for each social-religious-economic station of society are listed as follows.

1) Religious practitioners, scientists and educators should use light green.

2) Soldiers, administrators and bureaucrats should use bluish green.

3) Farmers, bankers and traders should use yellowish green.

4) Servants, laborers and workers should use dark green.

Venus Astral Talisman.
Flawless diamond handcrafted
in 18k gold. Piece no.1068

6. Venus (Shukra)

Venus is a beneficent planet which rules sex and sensuality, love and marriage, material comfort and luxury. Singers and dancers, artists and craftsmen, actors and prostitutes, and other professions involved in entertaining people are strongly influenced by Venus's sensual energy. A person with a strong Venus in his or her horoscope tends to have a happy marriage, enjoy material comforts, is optimistic and charismatic, makes others happy, and moves with physical grace and coordination. Diplomats and peacemakers are often governed by Venus. Venus is associated with flowers, jewels, and other beautiful objects, as well as semen, sweet foods and flavors, tropical climates, sexual activity, nice clothes, and various other sensual pleasures. People with a powerful Venus often experience distress of the excretory system due to overindulgence in food and drink.

When Venus is exalted one will be humanitarian, long-lived and possess many good qualities. But if the position of Venus in one's horoscope is weak or afflicted, one becomes vulnerable to loss of libido, impotence and sterility, venereal (lit. of Venus) complaints, and rapid aging. **Indigo** is the cosmic color transmitted by diamonds and other colorless gems. This color influences all watery elements in the body, especially mucous and sperm. Venus astral talismans are known to induce purity of body and mind, confer artistic talent and worldly happiness, strengthen the bones, and improve the quality of all bodily secretions, such as mucous, hormones, and semen.

Gemstones governed by Venus transmit its cosmic energy through diamonds, quartz crystals, zircons, goshenites, white topaz, white sapphires, and other colorless gemstones with clear transparency. Various subtle hues such as pink, yellow and blue tints are suitable for different types of professions and social positions, as long as the gem is void of solid color.

Note: As Venus is incompatible with the Sun, Moon and Jupiter, diamonds and other colorless gems should not be used with rubies, pearls and yellow sapphires. Specifically designed talismans like the *Nava-Ratna* (nine gems setting) are an exception to this principle.

From a rare depiction of Shukra, the Sanskrit name of Venus, here representing the white, clear jewels of this planet

The particular hue or type of tinted diamonds recommended for each desired social-religious-economic station of society are listed as follows:

1. Religious practitioners, scientists and educators should use white.

2. Soldiers, administrators, politicians and bureaucrats can use pinkish.

3. Farmers, bankers and traders should use yellowish.

4. Servants, laborers and workers should use blue to blackish.

Ketu Astral Talisman. Flawless cat's eye handcrafted in 18k gold. Piece no.321

7. Ketu (Moon's South Node)

Ketu is a mysterious planetary influence which, like *Rahu,* is malevolent and afflictive unless located in a powerful position or conjoined with a beneficent planet. *Ketu* governs theology, monastic life, crime and punishment, hidden enemies and dangers, and the occult. Unless correctly balanced, *Ketu* can cause poverty and other obstructions in one's life. *Ketu* is associated with suffering and the consequent aspiration for spiritual liberation.

If *Ketu* is exalted one will be wealthy and protected from evil. But if *Ketu* appears in a weak or harmful position in one's horoscope, one becomes prone to fatal diseases of a mysterious nature as well as compulsive gambling. **Infra-Red** is the cosmic color transmitted by cat's eye gems. Infra-red color waves are the hottest of all the cosmic rays and are known to be useful in many chronic and terminal illnesses such as cancer and all forms of paralysis. Infra-red color also aids digestive problems and skin diseases. *Ketu* astral talismans can also enhance psychic powers, confer protection from hidden enemies, and avert dangers such as drowning, intoxication, and criminal punishment. *Ketu* is also said to bring good luck to gamblers (if exalted).

Gemstones: ruled by *Ketu* include cat's eye chrysoberyl, beryl, apatite, tourmaline, fibrolite and other yellow to greenish-brown gems which display a strong chatoyant 'cat's eye' light reflection on the surface and often within the crystal when cabochon cut. These gems should also possess a high degree of transparency in order to properly transmit beneficial *Ketu* energy.

Note: As *Ketu* is incompatible with Sun, Mars and Moon, cat's eye gems should not be used with rubies, corals or pearls. Specifically designed talismans like the *Nava-Ratna* (nine gems setting) are an exception to this practice.

The particular hue or type of cat's eye color recommended for each social-religious-economic station of society are listed as follows:

1) Religious practitioners, scientists and educators should use honey yellow.

2) Soldiers, administrators and bureaucrats should use honey brown.

3) Farmers, bankers and traders should use honey green.

4) Servants, laborers and workers should use dark green.

From a rare depiction of the Vedic pantheon, Ketu, Descending Node of the Moon, here representing the cat's eye jewels of Ketu

*Saturn Astral Talisman.
Flawless, unburned blue
sapphire handcrafted in
18k gold. Piece no.68*

8. Saturn (Shani)

Saturn is a powerful planet whose position in one's horoscope strongly influences one's work and employment, as well as obstacles one must overcome in order to succeed in one's chosen field. Saturn is associated with the color blue, darkness, obstinacy, gambling, and chronic diseases. It governs aging and death, yoga practice, foreign travel, hunters and thieves. While malevolent by nature, when properly placed or balanced Saturn can also induce great virtues, such as compassion, charity, longevity, meditative insight, and positive public influence.

When Saturn is exalted one will be long-lived, charitable, lavish, proficient and an affectionate mate. But if Saturn is weak in a person's horoscope, one becomes vulnerable to headaches, neuralgia, and other disorders of the nervous system, as well as epilepsy, stupidity, and fainting. **Violet** is the cosmic color transmitted by blue sapphires and other natural blue to violet gems. Violet color waves are cold and related to Saturn, the planet which governs suffering and poverty. Saturn also rules the entire nervous system. Therefore, most diseases of the nerves, such as neuroses and nervous tension may be caused by an afflicted Saturn. Saturn being the slowest planet also causes diseases of a chronic nature and can cause delays if ill-disposed. Saturn astral talismans are known to help strengthen a person's nervous system. They also repel envy from others, avert demoniac influences, provide protection against dangers during travel, make one more serious and far-sighted, and induce mental tranquility.

Gemstones governed by Saturn transmit its cosmic energy through blue sapphire, blue spinel, tanzanite, indicolite, iolite, amethyst and other natural blue to violet gems with transparent clarity. Only flawless gems possess the capacity to properly transmit positive astral energy from Saturn.

Note: As Saturn is incompatible with Sun, Moon and Mars, Saturn gems such as blue sapphire should not be used with ruby, pearl or red coral. Specifically designed talismans like the *Nava-Ratna* (nine gems setting) are an exception to this principle.

From a rare depiction of Shani, the Vedic deity of Saturn, here representing the blue jewels of Shani

The particular hue or type of blue color recommended for each social-religious-economic station of society are listed as follows:

1) Religious practitioners, scientists, educators and women should use light blue.

2) Soldiers, administrators, leaders and bureaucrats should use violet blue.

3) Farmers, bankers and traders should use greenish blue.

4) Servants, laborers and workers should use gray to black blue.

Mars Astral Talisman.
Flawless coral handcrafted
in 18k gold. Piece no.159

9. Mars (Mangala)

Mars is a masculine planet which radiates an intense and fiery energy. Mars governs soldiers and warfare, ambassadors and orators, restaurateur and cooks, athletes and pilots, real estate and construction. It rules the color ochre-red, the metal element, vegetation, and the basic energy of life. The position of Mars in one's horoscope determines relations among brothers, courage and strength, vitality and sexual drive. When Mars is powerfully placed, a person becomes highly energetic and devotes his or her energy to constructive endeavors and worthy causes. When afflicted, Mars causes a person to behave erratically and waste energy on worthless pursuits. A severely debilitated Mars often indicates a violent temper and destructive tendencies.

When Mars is exalted one has great energy, is learned, well-known and regal, But if Mars is located in a weak or afflicted position in one's horoscope one becomes prone to boils (due to impure blood), unstable blood pressure, anemia, and violence. **Yellow** is the cosmic color transmitted by coral and other ochre colored gems. Yellow color waves are related to the lymph nodes, bone marrow, blood, and head. Mars astral talismans may help to strengthen these vital elements. They also help avert violence and warfare, moderate lust, improve finances, and reduce mental depression.

Gemstones ruled by Mars include natural coral, cornelian, and other pink to red ocher colored gems. As always, the use of fine quality gems, free of defects, is imperative for transmission of auspicious astral energy rays.

Note: As Mars is incompatible with Mercury and Saturn, Mars gems like red coral should not be used with emerald or blue sapphires. Specifically designed talismans like the *Nava-Ratna* (nine gems setting) are an exception to this principle.

From a rare depiction of Mangala, the Vedic ruler of Mars, here representing the ochre-red jewels of Mangala

The particular hue or type of reddish ochre color recommended for each social-religious-economic station in society are listed as follows:

1) Religious practitioners, scientists and educators should use pink red.

2) Soldiers, administrators, leaders and bureaucrats should use blood red.

3) Farmers, bankers and traders should use orange red.

4) Servants, laborers and workers should use brown red.

In order to transmit pure, unobstructed astral energy rays, gems must be free of flaws. Gems with defects are considered to have formed in a 'diseased' condition. Next we will see what the *Vedas* have to say about gemstone clarity.

Since the beginning of civilization man made efforts to depict creation in visual form. A papermaché globe from India, dating from the seventh century is a case in point. But the most powerful objects of this kind are the rare, pure crystals we so admire and respect. Millenia of experience have proven the crystals' extraordinary power to affect earthly events

IV
Gemstone Clarity

"Pure, flawless gems have auspicious powers which can protect one from demons, snakes, poisons, diseases, sinful reactions, and other dangers, while flawed stones are evil and inauspicious."

Garuda-Puranam:
chapter 68, verse 17

"A gem free from all impurities and radiating its characteristic internal luster should be looked upon as an "escort" of good luck. A gem which is cracked, fissured, devoid of luster, or appearing rough or sandy, should not be used at all."

Agni-Puranam:
chapter 246, verse 7 & 8

Here are ancient **Vedic references** from both the *Garuda Puranam* and the *Agni Puranam* which state emphatically that 'flawed' gemstones are inauspicious, while 'clean' gems are bringers of good fortune. **Note**: As they did not have high-powered microscopes in the ancient times it stands to reason that flawless means 'eye-clean'.

After many years of researching and experimenting with gemstones, it is our carefully considered opinion that the old *Vedic* texts are correct. Flawed gems are simply a source of misfortune, not to mention their being ugly! Think about it! How many people are prepared to tolerate 'defects' in their clothing, or any other personal items which they possess. Even a single scratch on a nice automobile is an eye-sore, so why do people tolerate flawed gems? How can one read through cracked eye-glasses?

Think of a gemstone like a radio crystal. The crystal receives and transforms the invisible radio sound waves into audible sound. If the crystal has even one defect the sound will be distorted and unpleasant.

As stated before, gemstones are natural transmitters on Earth of 'astral' energy waves radiated from the *Nava-graha* or nine planets recognized by the *Vedic* science of 'sidereal' astrology. It is common sense that only 'clean' gems will transmit 'undisturbed' astral energy waves

At present, the gem trade has lost much of its integrity because of the wide-spread treatment of natural gems to conceal or 'change' imperfections. Especially guilty are the emerald dealers who 'oil' flawed gems as a routine procedure (the oil enters the gem through internal cracks which break the surface of the stone). The gold smith (and the owner) are unaware of the defective condition which often results in broken stones. Even if the stones make it past the setter, the oil will dry out in a few years and the 'ugly' flaws will again become visible. This confuses the owner who may even think that the stone has been switched.

There **are** eye-clean, beautiful emeralds on this planet but they are scarce and costly. If one cannot afford the cost of an auspicious emerald then one can opt for an *upa-ratna* or 'secondary gem'. In place of emerald for the planet Mercury (*Budha-Graha*) one could use **tsavorite** (green grossularite), chrome-green or green **tourmaline**, chrome-green or green **diopside,** green **peridot** or **green jade.** Jade, being an 'aggregate' (made up of tiny crystals all fused together) is less preferable than the other Mercury gems which are 'single unit' crystals.

Along with the *Nava-ratna* or nine 'primary' gems, there are many other 'natural' gemstone choices based on color. These '*upa-ratnas*' are less expensive than their precious counter-parts and yet they conduct the same astral energy of their associated planet. They are also easier to find without flaws or treatment.

Here is a list of foremost *upa-ratnas* known to man, along with their ruling planets:

1) Red spinel, red garnet and red tourmaline (rubellite) are ruled by the Sun;

2) Moonstone is ruled by the Moon;

3) Yellow topaz, yellow beryl (heliodor), yellow tourmaline and citrine are ruled by Jupiter;

4) Orange zircon, spessartite and other orange garnets are ruled by *Rahu*;

5) Tsavorite, green tourmaline, diopside, green jade and peridot are ruled by Mercury;

6) White (colorless) sapphire, white topaz, zircon and quartz are ruled by Venus;

7) Beryl, fibrolite and tourmaline cat's eyes are ruled by *Ketu*;

8) Tanzanite (blue zoisite), blue spinel, cordierite, and amethyst are ruled by Saturn;

9) Cornelian and bloodstone are ruled by Mars

Remember: Whatever gems you use should be flawless, because according to ancient *Vedic* wisdom **only 'eye-clean' gems are helpful and attractive, while visibly flawed gems are defective and disturbing!**

Having described in brief the individual nature and powers of the nine planetary gemstones along with the *upa-ratnas* (semi-precious gems), we will now elaborate on their preparation and use as astrological talismans.

A list of other *Upa-Ratna* gemstones mentioned on the facing page.

Listed horizontally from top left to lower right:

Red spinel, red garnet, red tourmaline (rubellite), moonstone, albite moonstone.

Yellow topaz, yellow beryl (heliodor), citrine, orange zircon, spessartite.

Orange garnet, tsavorite, green tourmaline, diopside, peridot.

White sapphire, white topaz, zircon, quartz, 'tiger' eye.

Tanzanite, blue spinel, amethyst, cornelian, bloodstone.

This talisman ring, crafted in 18k yellow and white gold, features a fantastic, completely flawless 'Karkatana' or hessonite of seven carats to strengthen the Moon's North Node, Rahu. Also featured are a pair of flawless 'Sutra-mani' or cat's eyes of one carat to enhance the Moon's South Node, Ketu. Small diamonds grace the Rahu symbols on the sides for a 'touch of Venus'. The two tubes contain Rahu's sacred herb, 'Ashes of Cynodon dactylon' (Durva-bhasma), prepared in 1978 by the venerable Dr. Vajracarya, Chairman of the Nepal Ayurveda Association. This special ring is defined as 'panca-dhatu'or 'Five Great Elements': earth for the gem, water for the herb, fire for the metal, air for the symbol, and space (akasha) or ether for the number.

V

Astral Gemstone Talismans

"A reflection of the Sun may be experienced in place of the Sun, but it's illumination is never possible independent of the Sun."

Sri Chaitanya Charitamrita: Madhya-lila,
chapter 25, verse 117

A careful study of the foregoing information on the nature and cosmic influence of the nine planets in sidereal astrology will provide a better understanding of the astral power each planet exerts over the destiny of human beings. Furthermore, when one has determined through correct astrological calculations which planets exert the strongest influences over one's life, one can then manipulate these cosmic forces by the proper use of *kavacas* or astrological talismans.

Since ancient times sages and alchemists of the East have revealed the precise science relating the elements of nature with the nine planets, as well as the proper method of combining these astral elements into powerful talismans. This information was originally derived from ancient Vedic texts, and it was from these Oriental sources that Western alchemists and astrologers derived their knowledge, most of which was kept secretly confined to the initiated higher circles.

It is stated in the **Secret Teachings Of All Ages** by Manley Hall that, "The rays of the celestial bodies, striking the crystallizing influences of the lower world, become the various elements. Partaking of the astral virtues of their source, these elements neutralize certain unbalanced forms of celestial activity and, when properly combined, contribute much to the well-being of man."

The philosopher Agrippa has described in **Three Books of Occult Philosophy** the basic preparation of astrological rings as follows: "When any star (planet) ascends fortunately (i.e., located in an auspicious position in the horoscope), with the fortunate aspect or conjunction of the Moon, we must take a stone and herb that is under that star, and make a ring of the metal that is suitable to this star, and in it fasten the stone, putting the herb or root under it, not omitting the inscriptions of images, names and characters, as also the proper suffumigations."

Although currently displaced by the meaningless system of birthstones described in chapter II, the true science of 'planetary gemology' is still being practices by Asian (and some Western) astrologers. The ancient system of *panca-amrita*, – the five immortal nectars, is based simply on the proper combination of the planetary gemstone, metal, herb, symbol and number which corresponds to the planet that is to be enhanced. The *Vedic* process of *puja* or invocation of the planetary energy by means of a *mantra* (sound invocation) and *stotra* (prayer) represents the sixth *amrita* whereby the mind uses special sound vibrations.

After the talisman has been carefully prepared, one should first perform the appropriate rites of invocation & purification. On the appointed day and at the specified time one should immerse the gemstone-mounted talisman in either pure cow's milk (if available) or purified water; and while bathing it in sanctified incense smoke one should recite the *mantra* and *stotra* dedicated to the specific planet the appropriate number of times. Only then should one begin using their talisman.

On the following pages we have listed the necessary information and ingredients which are relevant to the preparation and use of planetary *kavacas* or talismans. Ancient texts do recommend certain gemstone carat weight limitations, so it is important to realise that larger gems are considered to be more powerful than smaller gems of the same fine quality. **Note:** For recommended gemstone color based on one's social-economic station refer to the previous chapter.

Sun Talismans

Planet to be strengthened:	Sun
Cosmic color to be enhanced:	Red
*Recommended gemstone:	Ruby
*Alternate gemstones:	Red spinel, garnet or rubellite
Solar/Lunar metal to be used:	Gold
Alternate metal:	Copper
Herbal ashes to be used:	**Milk weed** *(Arka-bhasma)*
Cosmic number to be used:	1
Planetary symbol to be used:	☉
Hand to be worn on (if a ring):	Right
Affected element:	Fire
Affected sense:	Sight
Affected bodily organ:	Eyes
Affected anatomical system:	Bone
Affected *chakra:*	5th, *Manipura*
Day for invocation;	Sunday
Time for invocation:	Sunrise

Mantra of invocation:

> *"Aum grinih suryaya namah."*
> (repeat seven times)

Stotra of invocation:

> *"Aum-japa kusuma samkasam kasya peyam maham dvitim, tamoram sarva papagnam pranato'smi divakaram."*

Sun Astral Talisman.
Flawless red spinel
handcrafted in 21k
gold. Piece no.60

Moon Talismans

Planet to be strengthened:	Moon
Cosmic color to be enhanced:	Orange
*Recommended gemstone:	Pearl
*Alternate gemstone:	Moonstone
Solar/Lunar metal to be used:	Silver
Herbal ashes to be used:	**Butia frandosa** (Palasa-bhasma)
Cosmic number to be used:	2
Planetary symbol to be used:	☾
Hand to be worn on (if a ring):	Left
Affected element:	Water
Affected sense:	Taste
Affected bodily organ:	Tongue
Affected anatomical system:	Blood
Affected *chakra:*	6th, *Svadtistana*
Day for invocation:	Monday
Time for invocation:	Evening
Mantra of invocation:	*"Aum som somaya namah."* (repeat 11 times)

Stotra of invocation:

> *"Aum dadhi sankha tusarabham*
> *chira-arnava samudbhavam,*
> *namami sasinam somam*
> *shambhor mukuta bhusanam."*

◆━━━━━━━━━━━━━

Moon Astral Talisman.
Handcrafted in 21k
gold. Piece no.268

Jupiter Talismans

Planet to be strengthened:	Jupiter
Cosmic color to be enhanced:	Light blue
*Recommended gemstone:	Yellow sapphire
*Alternate gemstones:	Yellow topaz, citrine or heliodor
Solar/Lunar metal to be used:	Gold
Alternate metal:	None
Herbal ashes to be used:	*Ficus religiosa* (Pippala-bhasma)
Cosmic number to be used:	3
Planetary symbol to be used:	♃
Hand to be worn on (if a ring):	Right
Affected element:	Ether
Affected sense:	Sound
Affected bodily organ:	Ears
Affected anatomical system:	Fat
Affected *chakra*:	2nd, *Ajna*
Day for invocation:	Thursday
Time for invocation:	One hour before sunset

Mantra of invocation:

"Aum brim brihaspataye namah."
(repeat 19 times)

Stotra of invocation:

*"Aum-devanam ca rishinam ca
gurum-kanja nasam-nibham,
budhyi bhutam trilokesam
tam namami brihaspatim."*

*Jupiter Astral Talisman.
Flawless citrine
handcrafted in 18k gold.
Piece no.340*

38

Rahu Talismans

Planet to be strengthened: Rahu
Cosmic color to be enhanced: Ultra-violet
*Recommended gemstone: Hessonite
*Alternate gemstones: Orange zircon and spessertine
Solar/Lunar metal to be used: Silver
Alternate metal: Iron
Herbal ashes to be used: ***Cynodon dactylon** (Durva-bhasma)*
Cosmic number to be used: 4

Planetary symbol to be used:

Hand to be worn on (if a ring):   Left
Day for invocation: Saturday
Time for invocation: 2 hours after sunset

Mantra of invocation: *"Aum ram rahave namah"*
                                    (repeat 18 times)

Stotra of invocation: *"Aum-ardhakaya maha-virya*
                        candra dvitya vimardanam,
                          simhika-garbha sambhutam
                      tam rahum pranamamy-aham."

*Rahu Astral Talisman. Flawless
hessonite with herb capsules
handcrafted in 18k gold.
Piece no.538*

Mercury Talismans

Planet to be strengthened: Mercury
Cosmic color to be enhanced: Green
*Recommended gemstone: Emerald
*Alternate gemstones: Green jade, peridot, green tourmaline, diopside, and tsavorite

Solar/Lunar metal to be used: Gold
Alternate metal: None
Herbal ashes to be used: *Achyranthes (Apamarga-bhasma)*
Cosmic number to be used: 5

Planetary symbol to be used: ☿

Hand to be worn on (if a ring):   Right
Affected element: Earth
Affected sense: Smell
Affected bodily organ: Nose
Affected anatomical system: Flesh
Affected *chakra:*   1st, *Sahasrana*
Day for invocation: Wednesday
Time for invocation: 2 hours after sunrise

Mantra of invocation: *"Aum bum budhaya namah."*
(repeat 9 times)

Stotra of invocation:

    *"Aum-priyangu kalika syaman
rupena pratimam budham,
    somyam somya guno petam
tam budham pranamamy-aham."*

Mercury Astral Talisman. Flawless diopside handcrafted in 21k gold. Piece no.126

Venus Talismans

Planet to be strengthened:	Venus
Cosmic color to be enhanced:	Indigo
*Recommended gemstone:	Diamond
*Alternate gemstones:	Colorless zircon, quartz, topaz, white sapphire, and beryl (goshenite)
Solar/Lunar metal to be used:	Silver
Alternate metal:	Platinum
Herbal ashes to be used:	*Ficus glomerata (Audumbara-bhasma)*
Cosmic number to be used:	6
Planetary symbol to be used:	♀
Hand to be worn on (if a ring):	Both
Affected element:	Water
Affected sense:	Taste
Affected bodily organ:	Lymph glands
Affected anatomical system:	Sperm
Affected *chakra:*	3rd, *Vishuddhi*
Day for invocation:	Friday
Time for invocation:	Sunrise

Mantra of invocation:

"*Aum shum shukraya namah*"
(repeat 16 times)

Stotra of invocation:

"*Aum hima kunda mrida labham
daityanam paramam gurum,
sarva sastra pravantaram
bhargavam pranamamy-aham.*"

◆────────────────────

Venus Astral Talisman. Flawless white sapphires handcrafted in 21k gold. Piece no.220

Ketu Talismans

Planet to be strengthened: Ketu
Cosmic color to be enhanced: Infra-red
*Recommended gemstone: Cat's eye chrysoberyl
*Alternate gemstones: Cat's eye apatite, tourmaline & beryl
Solar/Lunar metal to be used: Silver
Herbal ashes to be used: **Sacrificial grass** *(Kusa-bhasma)*
Cosmic number to be used: 7

Planetary symbol to be used: ☋

Hand to be worn on (if a ring): Right
Day for invocation: Thursday
Time for invocation: Midnight

Mantra of invocation: *"Aum kem ketave namah."*
(Repeat 18 times)

Stotra of invocation:

> *"Aum-palamsa puspa samkasam*
> *taraka graham-astakam,*
> *raudram raudrat makam-ghoram*
> *tam ketum pranamamy-aham."*

*Ketu Astral
Talisman. Flawless
beryl cat's eye &
white sapphires
handcrafted in
21k gold. Piece
no.158*

42

Saturn Talismans

Planet to be strengthened: Saturn
Cosmic color to be enhanced: Violet
*Recommended gemstone: Blue sapphire
*Alternate gemstones: Blue spinel, amethyst & indicolite
Solar/Lunar metal to be used: Gold
Alternate metal: Iron
Herbal ashes to be used: *Prosopis* (*Shami-bhasma*)
Cosmic number to be used: 8

Planetary symbol to be used: ♄

Hand to be worn on (if a ring): Right
Affected element: Air
Affected sense: Touch
Affected bodily organ: Skin
Affected anatomical system: Nervous
Affected *chakra:* 4th, *Anahata*
Day for invocation: Saturday
Time for invocation: 2 hours 40 minutes before sunset

Mantra of invocation: *"Aum sham shanaiscaraya namah."*
(repeat 23 times)

Stotra of invocation:
"Aum-nilanjana samabhasam
ravi-putra yama-agrajam,
chaya martanda sambhratam
tam namami sanaiscaram."

Saturn Astral Talisman. Flawless unburned blue sapphire handcrafted in 18k gold. Piece no.68

Mars Talismans

Planet to be strengthened:	Mars
Cosmic color to be enhanced:	Yellow
*Recommended gemstone:	Red coral
*Alternate gemstones:	Cornelian and bloodstone
Solar/Lunar metal to be used:	Gold
Alternate metal:	Silver
Herbal ashes to be used:	**Couch plant** (*Khadira-bhasma*)
Cosmic number to be used:	9
Planetary symbol to be used:	♂
Hand to be worn on (if a ring):	Right
Affected element:	Fire
Affected sense:	Sight
Affected bodily organ:	Genitals
Affected anatomical system:	Marrow
Affected *chakra:*	7th, *Muladhara*
Day for invocation:	Tuesday
Time for invocation:	1 hour after sunrise
Mantra of invocation:	*"Aum ang angarakaya namah."* (Repeat 19 times)

Stotra of invocation:

"Aum-dharani garbha sambhutam viddat kanti sama prabham, kumara-sakti hastam tam mangalam pranamamy-aham."

Mars Astral Talisman. Flawless coral handcrafted in 18k gold. Piece no.161

Nava-Ratna,
nine flawless
talisman gems
handcrafted in
21k gold. Piece
no.462

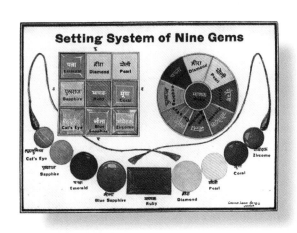

Rare sample of an
Indian gem chart
showing the correct
arrangement of the
Nine Gem Nava-
Ratna

Throughout the Orient, especially in India, Sri Lanka,
Thailand, and Burma (all ancient gemstone producers), special
importance has always been given to certain combination gemstone
talismans. the most well-known of these are the ***Nava-Ratna***
(9 gems), ***Sapta-Ratna*** (7 gems), ***Pancha-Ratna***
(5 gems), and the ***Tri-Ratna*** (3 gems).

Nava-Ratna

For countless centuries, the cultures of India and South-East Asia have revered the beautiful nine-gem talisman known as '*Nava-Ratna*'. Combining the gemstones representing each of the nine planets in sidereal astrology, the *Nava-Ratna* is esteemed by ancient tradition as a bringer of good fortune through its favorable influence on the planetary energies.
The most well-known design places a ruby, representing the Sun, in the center encircled by the other eight planetary gemstones, diamond for Venus, pearl for Moon, coral for Mars, hessonite for *Rahu* (the Moon's Ascending Node), blue sapphire for Saturn, cat's-eye for *Ketu* (the Moon's Descending Node), yellow sapphire for Jupiter and emerald for Mercury.

The following *stotra* may be recited before using the nine-gem talisman:

"Aum brahma murari, tripuranta-kari,
bhanu, shasi, bhauma-suto, budhasca,
gurusca, shukra, shani, rahu, ketu,
kurvantu sarve mama su pravatam."

"I invoke the Supreme Deity who is creator, maintainer,
and destroyer of the universe, and the deities presiding over the Sun,
Moon, Mars, Mercury, Jupiter, Venus, Saturn, and the shadow planets
Rahu and Ketu – May they bestow their benediction upon me."

Sapta-Ratna, the seven jewels talisman, combines the gems which correspond to the planets ruling the seven days of the week. Every day of the week is governed over by a specific planet. In many languages the days are named directly after the planet that rules over them. In English we must simply examine the Anglo-Saxon origin of the names of the days to see the correspondence. Sunday (Sun), Monday (Moon), and Saturday (Saturn) still remain intact. Tuesday (Mars) is derived from *Tewes,* the Anglo-Saxon name for Mars, god of war. Wednesday (Mercury) comes from *Woden's* day, the Anglo-Saxon name for Mercury, the messenger. Thursday (Jupiter) is from *Thor,* the Anglo-Saxon name for the lord of the demigods, Jupiter. And Friday (Venus) is from *Frides,* the Anglo-Saxon name for Venus, the deity of art, beauty, and material enjoyment. In practically every other language from Hindi to Thai the weekdays are directly named after their ruling planet.
The *Sapta-ratna* should be used as seven different rings or pendants to be worn successively on each corresponding day of the week. This practice is still popular in India, especially among astrologers, royal families and wealthy people.

Panca-Ratna combines the gemstones which represent a balance of the five material elements. Thus earth is represented by the green in emerald, water by the blue in sapphire, fire by the red in ruby, air by the yellow in topaz, and space by the absence of color in diamond. Another combination of the five gems has been described as gold for earth, pearl for water, ruby for fire, blue sapphire for air, and diamond for space.

The *Tri-Ratna* is a talisman believed to balance the three constituents of one's material body, crudely translated as marrow, mucus and air. These are represented by the three primary **cosmic colors** in nature – red, yellow and blue, or ruby, red coral and yellow sapphire.

In conclusion, we must again point out that gemstones selected for astrological and talismanic use should be flawless (eye clean), as defective stones are considered a source of misfortune. According to *Vedic* authority, the qualities of fire (color) and water (clarity) are the most important factors in choosing gems which are pure transmitters of benign planetary influence.

Nava-Ratna
Bona fide *Vedic* references regarding the Nine Planetary Gems

As I have done considerable research on this subject I request the readers to kindly consider the following bona fide *Vedic* references:

Adi-Guru, Srila Suta Goswami, has spoken the following words in the ancient **Garuda-Puranam**, chap.70, regarding the dawn of creation: "The blood of the great demon *Vala* was taken by *Surya,* the Sungod, who then fled into the blue vastness of space......*Rawana* attempted to block *Surya's* flight like a solar eclipse......appearing afraid of *Rawana,* the Sungod dropped the demon's blood, which fell down the deep pools of ancient *Bharata* (which included Burma, Siam, India, and of course Sri Lanka)......Beautiful and effulgent rubies, in all shades of color, possessing manifold virtues, originated on these shores.......the rubies from these fragrant lands are found in a variety of hues......some are like human blood, etc......being illuminated by rays of the Sun, this crystal species shines forth with wonderful color and brilliancy." **Note:** Here is a bona fide link between *Surya* and red rubies.

In chapter 69 it is further stated by *Suta Goswami:* "The teeth of the demon *Vala*......fell like stars into the oceans below and became seeds for a species of gems with the luster of full moon beams......entering into the shells of oysters......these seeds became pearls." Note: Another direct link that matches the nine planets *(Graha-Devas)* with associated gems.

There are nine foremost gems which are known as the **Nava-Ratna.** This quote attributed to the Sanskrit *'Brihat Jatak'* or Vast Production, (author and reference unknown) reads as follows:

> *Manikyam dinanayakasya vimalam muktaphalam*
> *shitagoh maheyasya cha vidrumam marakatam*
> *saumyasya-garutmakam/*
> *devejyasya cha pushparagam sura-achryasya vajram shaneh*
> *nilam nirmalamanyayoshcha gadite gomeda-vaiduryake//*

Translation: The Sun's gem is pure ruby, Moon is (natural) pearl, Mars is red coral, Mecury is emerald, Jupiter is yellow sapphire, Venus is diamond, Saturn is blue sapphire, *Rahu* is hessonite, and *Ketu* is cat's eye.

A slightly different version of this ancient *Sanskrit* verse is also quoted in the *'Mani-Mala'* page 575, verse 79 by *S. M. Tagore* (1879), and also in the ancient *'Parijataka'*, The Tree of Paradise, chapter 2, *sloka* 21 compiled by *Sri Vedyanath,* son of *Venkata-Dhari* (date unknown), and reads as follows:

> *Manikyam taraneh sujatyamamalam muktaphalam shitagoh*
> *maheyasya cha vidrumo nigaditah saumyasya-garutmatam/*
> *devejyasya cha pushparagam asura-achryasya vajram shaner*
> *nilam nirmalamanyayoshcha gadite gomeda-vaiduryake//*

Translation: The Sun's gem is pure ruby, Moon is (natural) pearl, Mars is red coral, Mercury is emerald, Jupiter is yellow sapphire, Venus is diamond, Saturn is blue sapphire, Rahu is hessonite, and Ketu is cat's eye.

Finally I would like to mention the ultimate *Vedic* authority, His Divine Grace *Srila A. C. Bhaktivedanta Swami Prabhupada,* who obtained and still is wearing a blue sapphire for his powerful Saturn influence, as advised by his personal *Jyotishacarya* in *Sridham Vrindavan.*

Top
The Queen Sirikit Nava-Ratna. Nine flawless gems set in 21k gold. Piece no.369

Center
Sapta-Ratna. A seven weekday gems collection of rings set in 18k gold

Left
Nava-Ratna. Nine flawless gems set in 21k gold. Piece no.437

Right
Nava-Ratna. Nine flawless gems set in 21k gold. Piece no.940

VI
Choosing Your Planetary Gemstone

After much research and practice, we have
developed the following method for selecting 'planetary gems'
based on one's **sidereal** horoscope:

1. We first look to one's *lagna* or **rising sign** and then check the lord of the rising sign
to see if it is in an auspicious condition in the *rasi* chart. If this is the case then we wholeheart-
edly prescribe the gemstone ruled by the *lagna's* lord. Example: If one has Leo rising we look
to the position of the Sun (lord of Leo) in the chart. If the Sun is posited in an auspicious sign,
e.g. sign of exaltation, own sign, trine, or at least a friendly sign, it will act in a beneficial way.
If any of these are the case then we may recommended ruby or another
'Sun jewel' as one's first gem choice.

A list of the primary rising sign gems is given as follows:

Rising Sign (*Lagna*)	Ruling Planet	Gemstone
Aries	Mars	Red coral
Taurus	Venus	Diamond
Gemini	Mercury	Emerald
Cancer	Moon	Pearl
Leo	Sun	Ruby
Virgo	Mercury	Emerald
Libra	Venus	Diamond
Scorpio	Mars	Coral
Sagittarius	Jupiter	Yellow sapphire
Capricorn	Saturn	Blue sapphire
Aquarius	Saturn	Blue sapphire
Pisces	Jupiter	Yellow sapphire

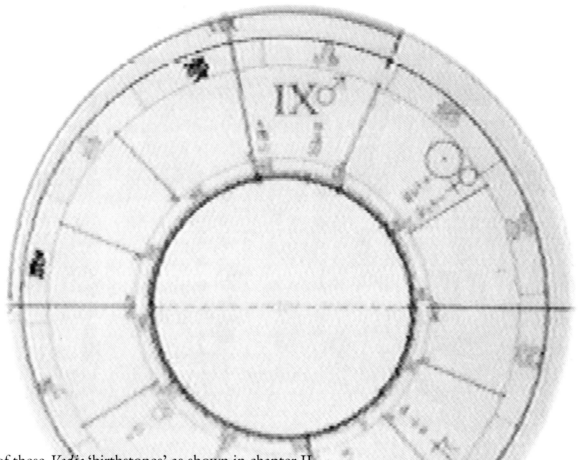

The list of these *Vedic* 'birthstones' as shown in chapter II is repeated again here for easy reference:

Birthstone	Ruling Planet	Moon Sign
Ruby	Sun	Leo
Pear	Moon	Cancer
Coral	Mars	Aries/Scorpio
Emerald	Mercury	Gemini/Virgo
Yellow Sapphire	Jupiter	Sagittarius/Pisces
Diamond	Venus	Taurus/Libra
Blue Sapphire	Saturn	Capricorn/Aquarius
Hessonite	Rahu	N/A
Cat's eye	Ketu	N/A

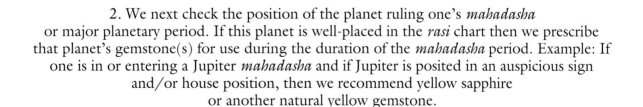

2. We next check the position of the planet ruling one's *mahadasha* or major planetary period. If this planet is well-placed in the *rasi* chart then we prescribe that planet's gemstone(s) for use during the duration of the *mahadasha* period. Example: If one is in or entering a Jupiter *mahadasha* and if Jupiter is posited in an auspicious sign and/or house position, then we recommend yellow sapphire or another natural yellow gemstone.

3. Next we look to one's birth sign or *Moon rasi,* i.e. the sign in which the Moon is positioned at the time of one's birth. In sidereal astrology the Moon's sign position is considered very important. Example: If one's Moon sign is Leo, a sign ruled by the Sun, then we must look to the sign and house position of the Sun in the horoscope. If the Sun is located in an auspicious position in the *rasi* chart then we can recommend a ruby or other red Sun jewel as one's 'birth stone.'

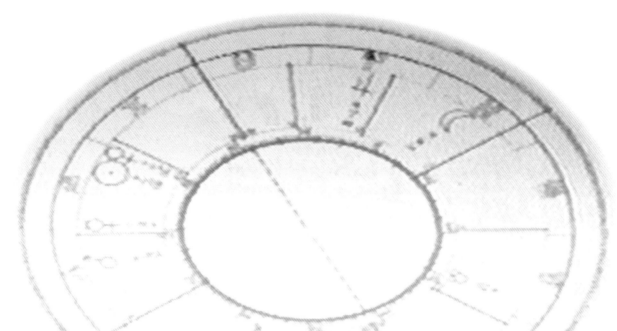

Following is a list of the 27 constellations, their ruling planet and corresponding gemstone:

BIRTH STAR	RULED BY	GEM
ASWINI	KETU	CAT'S EYE
BHARANI	VENUS	DIAMOND
KARTIKAI	SUN	RUBY
ROHINI	MOON	PEARL
MRIGASIRA	MARS	CORAL
ADRA	RAHU	HESSONITE
PUNARVASU	JUPITER	YELLOW-SAPPHIRE
PUSHYAM	SATURN	BLUE-SAPPHIRE
ASLESHA	MERCURY	EMERALD
MAGHAM	KETU	CAT'S EYE
POORVA-PHALGUNI	VENUS	DIAMOND
UTTAR-PHALGUNI	SUN	RUBY
HASTAM	MOON	PEARL
CHITRA	MARS	CORAL
SWATI	RAHU	HESSONITE
VISHAKAM	JUPITER	YELLOW-SAPPHIRE
ANURADHA	SATURN	BLUE-SAPPHIRE
JUSTHA	MERCURY	EMERALD
MOOLAM	KETU	CAT'S EYE
POORVASHADA	VENUS	DIAMOND
UTTARSHADA	SUN	RUBY
SRAVANA	MOON	PEARL
DHANISTHA	MARS	CORAL
POORVABADRAPADA	JUPITER	YELLOW-SAPPHIRE
UTTARBHADRAPADA	SATURN	BLUE-SAPPHIRE
REVATHI	MERCURY	EMERALD

4. We then check the *janma-naksatra* or the constellation in which the Moon is posited at birth. Each of these 27 birth stars is ruled by one of the nine planets recognized in sidereal astrology. Example: If one's birth constellation is '*punarvasu*' (the seventh constellation), which is ruled by Jupiter, then we look to the position of Jupiter in the horoscope. If Jupiter is located in an auspicious sign and/or house position in the *rasi* chart, then we can recommend yellow sapphire or another yellow 'Jupiter' jewel.

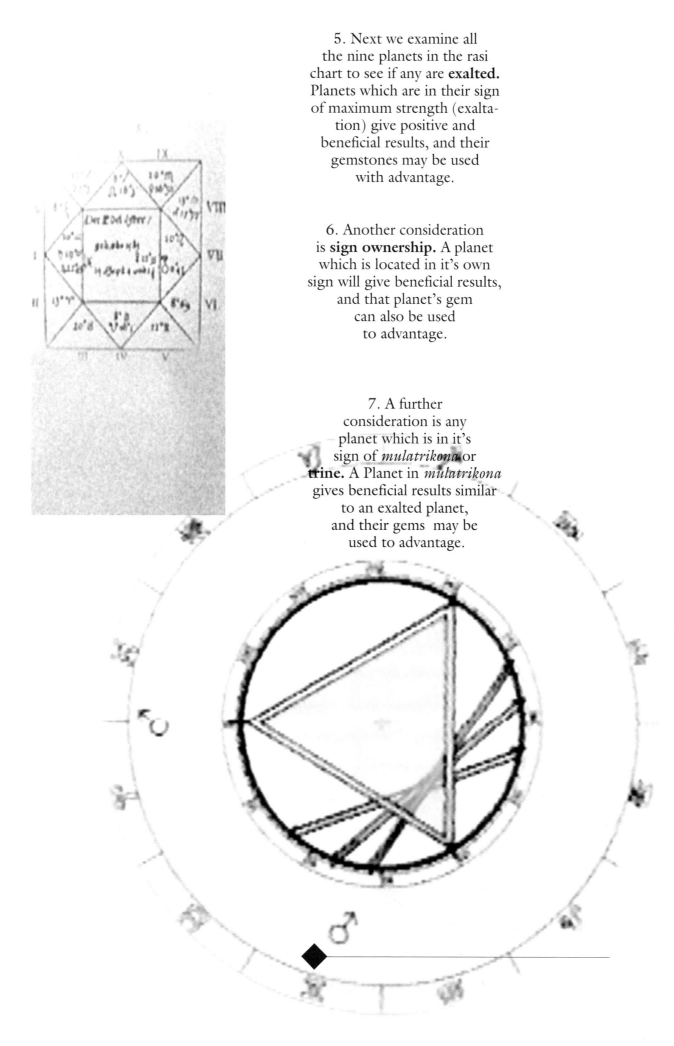

5. Next we examine all the nine planets in the rasi chart to see if any are **exalted.** Planets which are in their sign of maximum strength (exaltation) give positive and beneficial results, and their gemstones may be used with advantage.

6. Another consideration is **sign ownership.** A planet which is located in it's own sign will give beneficial results, and that planet's gem can also be used to advantage.

7. A further consideration is any planet which is in it's sign of *mulatrikona* or **trine.** A Planet in *mulatrikona* gives beneficial results similar to an exalted planet, and their gems may be used to advantage.

8. A planet which is located in a **friendly sign**
will also give beneficial results, and it's gemstone may be used to advantage.

9. Our final consideration is **preference** based on the characteristic 'planetary influence'.
Example: If a person wishes to use a Sun jewel like ruby or red spinel to increase their name
and fame, then we will recommend that stone provided the person's Sun is not located in
an unfriendly or inauspicious sign and/or house position in their *sidereal* horoscope.

Note: It is our practiced and well-considered opinion that fine, natural gemstones
do indeed 'strengthen' or magnify the influence of their associated planets. Therefore, lucky
planets equate lucky gems. If a person intends to wear their lucky gemstone then they should
only use gems which are related to planets that are considered to be 'lucky' or posited in an
auspicious *rasi* (zodiac sign) and/or *bhava* (house) in their sidereal birth chart. Gemstones **do
not** alter or change the angle, position or condition in which planets are placed in one's horoscope. Methods for propitiating or reducing the harmful effects of evil or malevolently placed
planets in one's birth chart include the chanting of planetary mantras, prescribed sacrifices and
charity. These may be performed along with the use of associated planetary gemstones to
help 'magnify' the prayer. A person who is unwilling to perform these meritorious
acts should not use gems for unlucky planets.

Important: Whichever planetary gemstones you choose **must be free of
visible flaws** in order **to properly transmit beneficial astral energy.** Even though there is
precious little direct information on the use of planetary gemstones in the *Vedic* texts, we do
have the following quote from the ancient *Agni-puranam*, (chapter 246, verses 7 & 8):

*"A gem free from all impurities
and radiating its characteristic internal luster
should be looked upon as an 'escort' of good luck.
A gem which is cracked, fissured, devoid
of luster, or appearing rough or sandy,
should not be used at all."*

With all these methods it is necessary to first cast a person's sidereal horoscope or *janma-patrika* (birth chart). This requires very expert calculations based on one's birth date, time and place. If one doesn't know their birth 'time' it is still possible to cast the horoscope accurately enough to see the planetary 'sign' positions (although this is much less precise in other areas). After casting the horoscope, look to see if any of the planets are in 'auspicious' rasi positions. All of these 'auspicious' sign positions give good results. According to B.V. Raman, India's leading astrologer, "A planet in it's **own sign** is rendered powerful to do good. A planet in it's **sign of exaltation** is rendered even more powerful to do good than in it's own sign. A planet in it's **sign of *mulatrikona*** is rendered powerful to do good similar to when in exaltation." Planets which are in **enemy signs** or which are **debilitated** usually have harmful or inauspicious influences. Professor *Raman* also states that planets which are debilitated give results opposite of when in strong sign positions. In other words, 'bad results'. (**Note**: There are certain astrological considerations which may 'cancel' harmful planetary positions; but it is the opinion of most sidereal astrologers that "once a bad planet, always a bad planet.")

An example may be taken from one of my own experiences with gem therapy. According to my Sidereal horoscope I have some exalted (strong) planets, some weak planets and some negative planets. Saturn in particular is already a *krura-graha* or cruel planet and it's position in my horoscope is even worse. Still, I was advised by some sidereal astrologers to use a blue sapphire, the gem for Saturn, in order to 'pacify' Saturn's harmful influence on me. This brings up the question of how gems should be chosen and what their effects will be. One group opines that gems should be used to 'pacify' harmful planets; another group believes that gems should be used to 'strengthen' weak planetary influences. While yet another belief is in 'strengthening' beneficial or auspicious planets. Let me relate my own experience and tell what my final conclusion is. Every Sidereal astrologer who has read my chart points out that Saturn in Cancer in the 12th house is quite malefic and is causing me many of the more long lasting problems in my life. I was advised to wear a blue sapphire to 'pacify' Saturn. After a long search I found a seven carat flawless, unburned, 'Brahmin' colored blue sapphire from Burma. I bought the gem, immediately had it set into a special gold ring, and on Saturday, two hours and forty minutes before sunset, I installed the ring after reciting the appropriate mantras.

Almost as soon as I started wearing this most auspicious blue sapphire I began having ill fortune. I started getting frequent headaches and my business started slowing down along with my energy level. Almost everything I did was beset with obstacles. Finally, after using the stone for almost one year, I took it off in frustration. Later I had the opportunity to show my birth chart to *Pandit Vidyadhar Shukla* (the Chief Brahmin Priest of Thailand) who confirmed that Saturn was indeed a 'bad influence' for me. He further suggested that as the blue sapphire had made matters worse, this was a good case against the theory that gems 'pacify' harmful planets. He suggested that I should wear a ruby to 'strengthen' the Sun in order to **counteract** Saturn's harmful influence. Since following this advise I have experienced much better effects on both my health, business and over-all outlook.

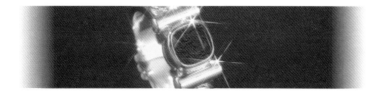

Considering my personal experiences as well as
the experiences of many friends, I have reached the conclusion that fine gems 'strengthen'
planetary influences, for better or worse, depending on each individual's horoscope. In
order to simplify matters I have created the following Planet/*Rasi* 'Strength & Weakness'
chart. Using this chart as intended will give a quick and easy look at the
most asupicious (and most inauspicious) planetary sign positions.

A.G.T. Planet / Rasi
'Strength & Weakness' chart

Read:
+10 =maximum strength
+7 =own sign
+5 =friendly sign
-10 =maximum weakness
-7 =enemy sign
-5 =unfriendly sign

	Aries	Taurus	Gemini	Cancer	Leo	Virgo	Libra	Scorpio	Sagittarius	Capricorn	Aquarius	Pisces
SUN	+10	-5	+5	+5	+7	+5	-10	-5	+5	-5	-7	-5
MOON	-5	+10	+5	+7	-5	+5	-5	-10	+5	-5	-5	+5
MARS	+7	-5	-5	-10	+5	-7	-5	+7	+5	+10	-5	+5
MERCURY	-5	+5	+7	-5	+5	+10	+5	-7	+5	-5	-5	-10
JUPITER	+5	-5	+5	+10	+5	-5	-5	-5	+7	-10	-5	+7
VENUS	-5	+7	+5	-5	-5	-10	+7	-7	+5	-5	+5	+10
SATURN	-10	+5	+5	-5	-5	+5	+10	-7	+5	+7	+7	+5
RAHU	*	+10	*	*	*	*	*	-10	*	*	*	*
KETU	*	-10	*	*	*	*	*	+10	*	*	*	*

*Since Rahu and Ketu are Aprakasha or 'shadow planets',
they reflect the qualities of the Lord of the sign they occupy. Example:
If Rahu is located in Virgo, a sign ruled by Mercury, you should
look to the position of Mercury in the chart and
predict similar results for Rahu.*

We welcome any input from readers
about their own experiences with flawless
gems and their astral powers

VII

Ancient Gemological Knowledge

THE Gemological Institute of America, which today poses itself as the paramount authority in the field of gemology, was founded less than 70 years ago.

For thousands of years, however, a sophisticated system of gemology has been practiced in the Orient. This knowledge is recorded in the Sanskrit language in specific *Vedic* Texts. Most of the principles governing this ancient gemological science are still practiced today, although modern scientific instruments have replaced trained eyes and fingers in the analysis and identification of gems. The basic methods, however, remain the same.

Following are some summary translations of original *Sanskrit* texts appearing in the *Garuda-puranam* (chapters 68 – 80), which pertain to the science of gemology. Due to its age (estimated to be over 5,000 years old), certain information may not be contemporarily relevant. But it is interesting to note the similarities between these ancient practices and modern methods of gem testing.

Introduction

The Legend of Vala

Vedic Text

Sri Suta Goswami said: I shall now expound the science of gemology. Long ago, in ancient times, there lived a great demon name *Vala*. Overpowering the King of Heaven, *Indra, Vala* became the tyrannical ruler of the entire universe. By deceit, however, the oppressed demigods tricked *Vala* into acting as the sacrificial animal in a ritual performance. But once *Vala* was tied to the sacrificial stake, the demigods suddenly abandoned their mock sacrifice, and immediately killed the powerful demon.In fact, for the benefit of the demigods and the universe, *Vala* had allowed himself to be slain.

the demigods then severed his various limbs which transformed into the creative seeds of precious gems. As the potent body of *Vala* was dismembered, a tumultuous roar sounded through the celestial regions, and all the deities, demons, mystics, and serpent-gods anxiously rushed to gather up the gem seeds. The demigods clamored to secure the gem seeds, but the shock waves generated by their celestial chariots pushed some of the mystical essences down into the earthly sphere.Some of these seeds fell into rivers, some into the oceans, and some into the forests and mountains. There they germinated as mother lodes of the various gems, each one imbued with its own intrinsic potency.

All these gems possess talismanic powers. The fine, auspicious stones can counteract poison, snake venom, diseases, and other dangers. Poor quality, inauspicious gems act in the opposite manner.Ruby, emerald, blue sapphire, cat's eye, yellow sapphire, diamond, pearl, hessonite, coral, bloodstone, quartz, jade, and red garnet are the foremost species of gems, and they should be selected only under the expert guidance of a learned gemologist.

The value of a gemstone is established by reference to the authoritative gemological texts. Quality is analyzed according to weight, cut, color, and clarity.

Ruby

Vedic Text

The blood of the high and mighty demon *Vala* was taken by *Surya*, the Sun-god, who then fled into the blue vastness of space. *Ravana*, the great king of Sri Lanka, who was puffed up with his power and his victory over the demigods, attempted to block the Sun-god's flight in the sky like a solar eclipse. Appearing terrified of *Ravana's* fearsome presence, the Sun-god dropped the demon's blood, which fell down into the deep pools of *Bharata* which were surrounded by forests of betel nut trees and scintillating with sunlit waves. (*Bharata* or ancient India, as referred to in the text, included Burma, Siam, Afghanistan, Pakistan, Nepal, Tibet and of course, Sri Lanka.)

From that time on, these pools became as holy as the sacred Ganges River and were known as *Ravana-Ganga*. The banks of these waters became covered with precious gemstones, all sparkling with dazzling splendor. Beautiful and effulgent rubies, as well as other colors of corundum, possessing manifold virtues, are the gemstones which originated on the perfumed shores of *Ravana-ganga*.

The rubies from these fragrant lands are found in a variety of hues. Some are red like human blood, while others resemble the red of pomegranate seeds. Some rubies are vermillion red and others are yellowish-red like saffron or shellac dye. These should be evenly colored with light shining from their very core. Being illuminated by rays of the sun, this crystal species shines forth with wonderful color and brilliancy, reflecting in all directions and spreading rays all around.

Kuruvinda rubies are not so purely colored as those rubies of the "top crystal" quality and are somewhat lacking in clarity and luster. (According to Apti's Sanskrit/English dictionary, both *kuruvinda* and *padmaraga* are names for ruby. But in the context of this book *kuruvinda* refers to rubies of inferior color and clarity while *padmaraga* denotes rubies that possess the finest (purest, unmixed) color and top crystal clarity. In this text, rubies of the finest quality are called *padmaraga*, 'lotus-hued' while poorer quality rubies are referred to simply as *kuruvinda* 'corundum'. It may also be noted here that the English name for corundum was derived from the ancient Sanskrit world *kuruvindam*).

The most important features of a 'top crystal' quality ruby are: (1) purity of color, (2) heavy specific gravity, (3) coldness of touch, (4) flawless and transparent clarity, (5) brilliancy and (6) excellent proportions.

The value of a ruby is based primarily upon the purity of color and its brilliancy. Any decreases in either of these qualities causes a proportionate decrease in value. The potency of a high-quality ruby is such that even an ignorant person living a sinful life and surrounded by deadly enemies is saved by wearing such a gem. Anyone wearing such a naturally effulgent ruby would be freed from diseases caused by any imbalance of the bodily functions.

Faults that characterize lower quality rubies are: A coppery tinge, silky inclusions, cloudy or oily appearance, dullness, off-color and excessive darkness around the edges (girdle) when the stone is held between the fingers (covering table and culet).

A potential ruby of exceptional quality should first of all be tested for specific gravity against a known ruby of the same size. A specimen which proves to be considerably lighter than the genuine ruby indicates that it belongs to another mineral species. In a situation where the results of testing proved inconclusive, one should use the scratch test, scratching the specimen with a known ruby. No other mineral except diamond or corundum can scratch a piece of genuine ruby or sapphire.

A genuine ruby possessing all auspicious qualities should not be worn together with a gem of imperfect or flawed features or one belonging to a species that is astrologically incompatible with it.

*The crystallized blood of
Vala. A perfect Sun
jewel set in a uniquely
designed ring. Flawless
ruby handcrafted in 18k
gold. Piece no.333*

One is advised not to wear a gem of poor quality or that is incompatible even if it
is set together with the divine *Kaustabha* jewel. For as a host of saints lose their status by
association with a single impure outcast, in the same way even one low quality or incompatible
stone can spoil and entire setting of precious gems.
A ruby, although genuine, should not be worn if it has strong color banding, excessive
inclusions within like numerous internal cracks, a sandy appearance, a rough surface, or is dull
and lusterless. Anyone using such a flawed ruby, even out of ignorance,
will suffer from disease, or loss of fortune.

Pearl

Vedic Text

The teeth of the great demon *Vala*, scattered throughout the celestial regions, fell like stars into the oceans below and became seeds for a species of gems with the luster of full moon beams. Entering into the shells of oysters lying within the ocean depths, these seeds became pearls. Oyster pearls found along the coasts of Sri Lanka, Bengal, and Persia, Indonesia and other lands located in the Southern Hemisphere are superior in shape, color, size, and other qualities to those from other countries.

Besides oyster pearls there are seven other types found in conch shells, wild boars' heads, elephant heads, king cobra's heads, bamboo stems, clouds, and fish heads. Pearls from elephant heads, bamboo stems, boar heads, fish mouths, and conch shells are lusterless, even though possessed of other auspicious qualities. Pearls from conch shells are usually the size of a large *kona* (the large end of a drum stick), and they possess a color similar to their host shell. Fish pearls are perfectly round and symmetrical. They possess a yellowish hue like the scales of the *pathenam* fish which often inhabit the mouths of deep sea whales. Boar pearls are colored like a boar's tusks and are found only in remote parts of the world. Such pearls are auspicious symbols of the *Varaha* boar-Incarnation of the Supreme Lord, *Sri Vishnu*.

Pearls derived from bamboo appear like hailstones in color, and they are found only within bamboo that has grown in a region populated by religious people. Pearls from the cobra's hood are perfectly round, like fish pearls, and they radiate a natural effulgence. By repeated washing, a snake pearl becomes as lustrous as a polished sword blade. Anyone possessing such a *naga-mani* attains rare good fortune, and even attains piety, luck, and eventually becomes illustrious as a leader of men, complete with a great collection of all precious gems.

Upon acquiring such a snake pearl, the owner should have the rite of installation performed by a priest who is learned in religious formalities. After hearing from the owner how the pearl was obtained and conducting the benedictory ritual, the priest should formally install the jewel inside the owner's house. On such an auspicious occasion, the sky becomes filled with dark and heavy rain clouds, thunder, and flashing lightning, such as exhibited at the time of universal dissolution. A man in possession of such a snake pearl will never be troubled by snakes, demonic beings, diseases, or disturbances in any form.

Cloud pearls, being naturally effulgent like the Sun, illuminate the sky in all directions and dispel the darkness of cloudy days. Glowing brighter than the combined light of the Moon, the twinkling stars, and fire, a cloud-born pearl dissipates even the darkest night exactly like the sunrise. A cloud pearl is so priceless that the entire earth, with her oceans filled with countless jewels and covered in layers of gold, would not be equal in value. Cloud pearls rarely reach this earthly world, because they are usually taken away by the demigods.

Even a low born man would become supreme ruler of the entire world if, as result of some past pious actions, he were to come into possession of such a pearl. The appearance of such a man on earth who obtained a cloud pearl during his lifetime would bring good fortune not only to himself, but to the entire human race as well. No form of evil could even touch the land within an 8,000 mile radius of his birthplace. An expert gemologist should appraise pearls according to their size, shape, and other qualities, rather than their place of origin.

Oyster pearls are the only type capable of being drilled through their centers. This is the method used for drilling pearls: First, the pearls should be mixed in bowl of rice previously soaked in lime juice. After simmering for some time on low heat, the pearls should be removed and rubbed with cool boiled rice water. After soaking, they should be pierced through the center.

AGT recommends the use of a perfect moonstone instead of cultured pearls as astral talismans for their jewelry as it is practically impossible to obtain astrologically effective natural pearls anymore.
High quality moonstones are a perfect replacement for the pearl of old.

This Moon Astral Talisman ring is piece no.127, a moonstone set with small diamonds in 18k gold

To clean pearls they should be kept in a covered clay container and lightly boiled in either milk, water, or wine. Thereafter, they should be carefully rubbed in a piece of pure linen cloth until they regain their natural luster. This process of cleaning pearls was taught by the great *Vyadhi* (*Vyadhi* was, according to the *Sanskrit* dictionary of *V.S. Apte*, a celebrated grammarian. *Vyadhisa* is a name for Lord *Vishnu*, most probably His *Dhanvantari* incarnation, in which form the Lord revealed the medical science to mankind. This latter meaning seems more suitable to this verse), out of his compassion
for the learned and virtuous.

Pearls worn by either kings or men of noble rank should be kept in a glass container, soaking in a solution of mercury and gold. This is the process followed by pearl experts in Sri Lanka. The test for a genuine pearl is to soak the specimen overnight in a mixture of warm oil and salt. The natural pearl will remain unaffected. Another test is to rub the specimen pearl with a piece of dry cotton cloth and rice. A genuine pearl will not lose
its color or luster in any way.

A pearl of the highest quality should be white, translucent, round in shape, lustrous, and of good weight and size. A large, round white pearl with effulgent luster and with a clean, even hole drilled through its center, which charms even a person who is not even interested in pearls, should be considered as possessed of a rare, good quality. The owner of such a pearl will never suffer any form of ill fortune.

Jupiter Astral Talisman. Flawless yellow beryl handcrafted in 21k gold. Piece no.371

Yellow Sapphire

Vedic Text

The skin separated form *Vala's* dismembered body was
transformed into mystic seeds from which originated yellow sapphires.
These fell primarily upon the lands crowned by the Himalayas and there formed mines
of these wonderfully endowed gems. Sapphires of white or light yellow color are known as
pusparaga. Those which are orange are called *kauranda*. Other auspicious colors are golden
yellow, rich yellow and greenish yellow sapphire. Yellow sapphires must be evenly colored,
flawless and well shaped in order to be considered auspicious.
The value of this gem is the same as a cat's eye of equivalent color and clarity.
The primary potency inherent in this gem is for blessing a woman with child birth even
if she has had difficulty. Also, as the energy of Jupiter, yellow sapphires confer happiness and
prosperity upon those advised to wear them by a competent astrologer.

Hessonite

Vedic Text

Fingernails of the great demon *Vala* were transformed into seeds of *Karketana* or hessonite gems, which are the rarest of the planetary jewels. Winds blew these hessonite seeds into the lotus ponds of Sri Lanka, India, and Burma.

The ideal color for hessonite is an intense orange hue appearing like a mixture of honey, blood and moonlight with a brilliant copper-colored sparkle.

Hessonites which are flawed, lack luster, or white or bluish in color are considered inferior and inauspicious. Hessonites of poor quality are common, while fine pieces are so rare that the ancients considered them the most blessed of all gems in the world. A pure hessonite sparkling with internal fire and set in a golden ornament is the ultimate talisman, capable of increasing the life span, the progeny, and the happiness of its owner. It can also remove evil thoughts and motives from the owner's mind. Any man possessing such a praiseworthy hessonite, even if only for ornamental purposes would surely become wealthy and famous in this lifetime.

Other gems which appear similar to hessonite, such as orange zircon, can be separated by their differences of refractive index, specific gravity, and other gemological characteristics. The market value of fine quality hessonite should be determined by a gem expert with special emphasis given to size, quality and origin.

Rahu and Venus
Astral Talisman. Flawless
hessonite and diamonds pendant
handcrafted in 21k gold.
Piece no.155

Emerald

Vedic Text

The bile of the great demon *Vala* was taken by the serpent king, *Vasuki* who split the heavens in two with one sweep of his mighty tail. With hood bedecked with jewels, his long body appeared like a bridge across the expanse of the heavens.

At that time, *Garuda*, the eagle-king carrier of the Supreme lord *Vishnu* and the sworn enemy of serpents, came flying through the heavens and blocked *Vasuki* with his mighty claws. Upon seeing *Garuda*, *Vasuki* became so afraid that the he dropped *Vala's* bile to the earth near the beautiful forests and perfumed trees of Mt. *Manikya*. (Since the mountain ranges of South Africa and South America are the world's foremost producers of emeralds, one explanation would be that Mount *Manikya* consisted of the combined areas of these two continents prior to their separating.) It also descended upon the landlocked areas beyond the Himalayas. (Most probably present day Afghanistan and Pakistan).

This bile transformed into the seeds of emeralds, and wherever it fell there originated mines of emeralds. Seeing this, *Garuda* picked up some of these emerald-seeds, but their power was so great that even he was overcome with a fainting spell causing him to scatter small quantities in several areas.

The finest colors of emeralds are compared to the following elements in nature: the green color on the neck of a parrot; the color of a flower called in Sanskrit, *Shirisha*; a blade of green grass; the color of fresh moss; the green found in a peacock's feather; the green on the back of a fire-fly. Anyone possessing fine quality emerald of any of these shades of green is blessed with great good fortune.

Most of the areas where *Vala's* bile fell, although exceptionally lush and beautiful, are rugged and hardly accessible. But the fine emeralds of these areas possess mystical powers, even to neutralize the poison of a king cobra.

Ancient Indian gemologists have given the highest praise to emerald possessing the following qualities: display a rich, even color; emit a soft glow; appear to glisten with gold dust inside; devoid of any serious internal or external blemishes. the gem also should be properly cut so that maximum light is refracted to the eye of one viewing it face up.

The emerald of superlative quality shines like green lightning and brings joy at first sight. Of second quality is one colored grass green, flawless, but with lighter tone and appearing transparent in the center (windowed). Dark colored emeralds showing little glow or fire should be considered inferior to those before mentioned.

Emeralds considered inauspicious are blackish, devoid of luster, appearing dirty inside or dried and brittle. Anyone concerned with their own well-being should never purchase or wear any oiled, dyed, or treated emerald. Also, emeralds of mixed colors are strictly forbidden. Emeralds which are too light green are not considered true emeralds, but are called green beryl.

Emerald substitutes can be detected by differences in specific gravity and refractive index. Simply by sight and touch experienced gemologists can discern these differences. Emeralds should be mounted in yellow gold, and worn, both by the doctor and patient, during the treatment of any disease, especially those caused by poison or an imbalance of the body's vital airs.

Top quality emeralds are deemed more valuable than a ruby of equal quality, while low quality emeralds are less valuable than comparable rubies.

*"The astrologer should use common sense - direct people away from their weaknesses and towards their strengths. For example, if debilitated Mars is in the second house and a person is having financial problems, don't advise them to go into the construction business, which is ruled by Mars (coral). Find a strength in the chart and push them in that direction; for example, exalted Venus in the tenth house could bring success in the entertainment or clothing business (diamond)."**

Mercury Astral Talisman. Flawless green tourmaline handcrafted in 18k gold. Piece no.206

*Ref. 'How To Read Your Horoscope', pg.280, para.2 by *H.G. Nalini-Kanta Dasa*.The *Vedic* Cultural Association, 51 Coelho Way, Honolulu, Hawaii 96817. 1987

◆

Diamond

Vedic Text

Wherever *Vala's* bone fragments fell, they geminated diamond crystals of various types. Consequently, diamonds are found in the following colors: slightly brownish, white as the full moon, blackish like a rain cloud, coppery-hued, dark yellow, bluish, greenish, pink, and light yellow.

Particular demigod preside over exceptionally fine diamonds of various colors. White diamonds of this standard are ruled by *Varuna*, Lord of the Oceans. Yellow diamonds are ruled by *Indra*, the Heavenly King. The *Maruts*, the Windgods, rule copper-hued diamonds, the greenish diamonds are ruled by *Surya*, the Sungod. The Firegod, *Agni*, rules brown-colored diamonds, and blue tinged diamonds are ruled by the Lord of Ancestors, *Aryama*.

Flawless, high-grade diamonds confer good fortune upon their wearers, whereas flawed diamonds are invariably a source of misfortune. Although a diamond may appear flawless internally, if any of its natural crystal edges appear fractured, or if it possesses an abraded, withered, or rough surface, it should not be kept within one's household, for it can cause numerous ills. Anyone wearing a seriously flawed or clouded diamond which refracts a reddish glimmer from defective facet edges, will surely be abandoned by the goddess of fortune. A diamond containing red spots will bring ruin.

A flawless diamond with an even outside and smooth symmetrical facets, and a high degree of dispersion is rarely to be found even upon royal crowns. Rough diamonds are generally hexagonal (cubical), octagonal, and dodecahedral, and exhibit external growth markings and sharply angled facets. If one owns a rough diamond with a well-shaped crystalline formation, high transparency and brilliancy, and devoid of any blemishes or visible inclusions, he acquires the following virtues: prosperity, longevity, marital happiness, children and livestock, and good harvests.

Auspicious diamonds help protect the wearer from attack by poisonous serpents, tigers, thieves, and deadly poisons. They protect his possessions from fire and flood and cause his complexion to become lustrous.

Diamonds should not be worn by women, because they possess a mystic potency that causes women to become unhappy.

Why diamonds are bad for women

by *Pandit Vidyadhar Sukla*
Chief Hindu Priest & Astrologer of Thailand

According to the *Shastras* (*Vedic* authority). such as *Garuda Purana,* diamonds should not be worn by women! In support of this dictate I would like to present my own opinion. Diamonds are ruled by the planet Venus (*Sukra*) who is the lord of Sexual Power and Beauty. If women wear diamonds it will increase their beauty and make them more attractive to men. This often causes men to lose control of themselves and commit sinful activity.

Diamonds abnormally increase a women's sexual desire. This can lead to their being damaged both mentally and physically.

Diamonds are the hardest element known to man. A woman who wears a diamond for a long time will become hard-hearted and unable to give proper affection to her husband and children.

In summary, it should be noted that women in ancient times did not wear diamonds weighing more than half a carat. Instead they used only small diamonds as accent stones in theit jewelry. The power of diamonds are exactly in proportion to their size.

Pandit Vidyadhar Sukla
Dated: 12. February, 1991

Venus Astral Talisman.
Flawless diamond handcrafted
in 18 gold.
Piece no.1067

Only a king is privileged to wear fancy colored diamonds of yellow, chartreuse, or pink colors. Their use by anyone in a lower station of life could prove harmful. A king wearing a diamond that flashes rays of light like bolts of lightning will surely be able to conquer other rulers and gain sovereignty over their wealth and followers.

Because there are various diamond substitutes such as white topaz, zircon, hessonite, white corundum, chrysoberyl, quartz-crystal, and also man-made imitations like glass, it is important that all diamond specimens be tested for genuineness by qualified gemologists who are expert in the science of identifying and appraising precious gems.

Before purchasing a diamond it should be positively identified through such tests as hardness and specific gravity. A genuine diamond, the hardest of all elements, cannot be scratched by any other metal or gemstone.

The value of diamonds depends more on color and clarity than total weight. Diamonds, because of their high refractive index, have the greatest reflective luster of any gem.

Cat's Eye

Vedic Text

Being arrested and bound by the demigods, *Vala* emitted a thunderous war cry.
This war cry transformed into the seed of the gem cat's eye.
Falling into the sea, these seeds agitated the ocean and produced huge waves which washed them upon the shore of nearby lands. Wherever they settled they formed mines of shimmering cat's eye. Many of these mines are near Sri Lanka's famous Vaidurya Hill and so the gems came to be known as *Vaidurya* stones. That terrible war cry of *Vala* also carried heavenward and impregnated the clouds and the sky. Later, carried to earth by rain and comets, these seeds formed smaller mines of cat's eyes in scattered areas.
The most precious cat's-eyes are golden green like the breast feathers of the peacock or light honey-green like a bamboo leaf. When these primary colors are mixed with shades of brown or burgundy, the gem is less valuable.
Gems such as apatite, tourmaline, and enstatite are sometimes mistaken for true chrysoberyl cat's eyes, but can be differentiated by their lesser hardness. Other imitations, such as glass or quartz, are easily detected by their relative lightness or low specific gravity.
The value of a true cat's eye varies according to its color, clarity, and shape. A cat's eye of excellent quality mined near the sea in Sri Lanka should be considered more valuable than an ordinary cat's eye. The value of cat's eye is approximately one third the value of similar quality blue sapphire.

Blue Sapphire

Vedic Text

The eyes of the great demon *Vala* were colored and shaped like the blossom petals of the blue lily flower. His eyes transformed into the seeds of blue sapphire gems and fell down on the sacred land of *Sinhala* (Sri Lanka) and the surrounding tropical areas of Southeast Asia. These sapphire seeds fell in such abundance that these lush and beautiful lands glowed with dazzling splendor.

The finest color of blue sapphire is compared to the blue mountain flowers which grow wild in Sri Lanka. These flowers are so sweet that they attract hoards of bumblebees and parrots eager to drink their nectar. blue sapphires of fine, evenly distributed color, free from flaws and cut to proper proportions for brilliancy are the most valuable. When blue sapphires have a green or violet tint, are slightly grayish or darkish-blue, or are colored light-blue like the sky, they are of medium value.

Blue sapphires that are excessively dark, light, or uneven in color, possessing a pronounced grayish tone, internal inclusions, external blemishes, visible black spots or internal feathers, are of low quality. Sapphires lacking brilliance due to poor proportions are also less valuable.

Both ruby and blue sapphire are of the same mineral species, corundum, with only the coloring agent differing. Therefore the same methods of identification established for ruby also apply to blue sapphire. Blue sapphires should never be subjected to burning for improving their color and clarity, as misfortune will certainly befall anyone doing so. Blue glass, lapis lazuli, blue spinel and other gems occasionally look like blue sapphires, but are easily detected by testing for hardness, specific gravity, and brightness.

The most rare and valuable of all blue sapphires is the *maha-nila*, which, when immersed in 100 times its own weight of milk, can tinge the milk blue. Astrologically, fine blue sapphires are as powerful as excellent rubies, but monetarily they are valued at one-quarter the price of a ruby of equal quality.

*Saturn Astral Talisman.
Flawless, unburned
blue sapphire,
handcrafted in 18k gold.
Piece no.114*

Coral

Vedic Text

The intestines of *Vala* were taken by the celestial serpent *Vasuki*, who deposited them
in oceans around the globe. They transformed into the original seeds of coral
which grow within the seas.
The best coral is colored either blood-red or pink-red. Other colors are dull-red, orange,
pink, pink-orange, white, black and chocolate brown. A well polished, bright coral with rich,
soothing dark-red color and without flaws is considered most auspicious. It possesses
power to increase the riches and wheat supplies of its wearer and also removes
obstacles and dangers.

Mars Astral Talisman.
Flawless coral
handcrafted in 18k gold.
Piece no.351

Red Garnet

Vedic Text

The toenails of *Vala* were transformed into red garnet seeds. These gem seeds were worshiped by the snake-gods who carried them in their mouths and dropped them in the lands surrounding the Himalayas, where garnet mines then originated.
Although found in a variety of colors, shades of red are the most common with blackish-red, reddish-brown, and orange-brown being the most prominent. As with rubies, garnets colored like the petals of the red lotus are considered the rarest and most beautiful and possess the mystic virtue of increasing both the wealth and progeny of their owners.

Sun Astral Talisman.
Flawless red garnet
handcrafted in 21k gold.
Piece no.880

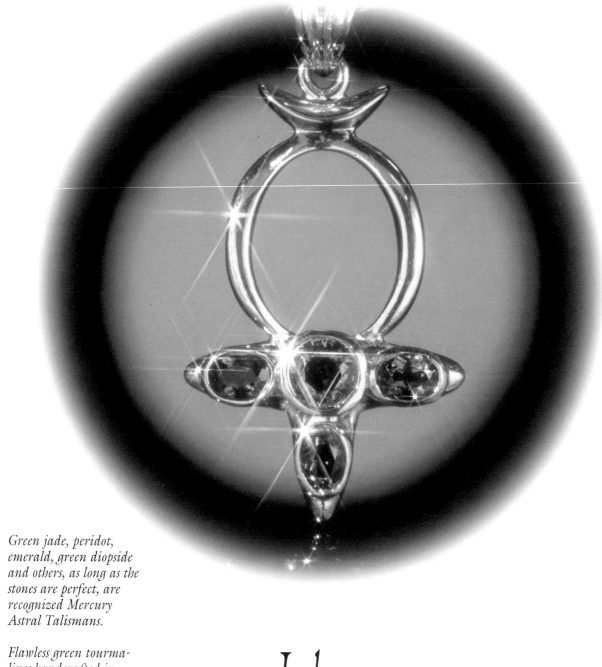

Green jade, peridot, emerald, green diopside and others, as long as the stones are perfect, are recognized Mercury Astral Talismans.

Flawless green tourma-lines handcrafted in 21k gold. Piece no.438

Jade

Vedic Text

Lord *Balarama* scattered the fat of *Vala's* body over the areas of China, Nepal, and the lands of the *Yavanas* and Mongols. Everywhere they fell, these transformed particles of fat originated deposits of jade.
Jades are primarily conch shell white or lotus stem green, but also are found in pink, lavender, and black colors.
Jade is extremely hard and resists scratching. It is difficult to cut, so a jade piece, beautifully cut and polished is worth far more than a similar gem in its natural rough shape.
Among all gems, fine quality jade has the greatest ability to remove negative karmic reactions.

Rock Crystal

Vedic Text

The potent semen of *Vala* transformed into the seeds of quartz (rock crystal).
These seeds germinated primarily in the Himalayas and the lands to their north.
The crystals are usually transparent and colorless, and are often so brilliant
that they are mistaken for diamonds.
Any one respectfully wearing a pure quartz crystal set in gold will attain good fortune in this
life and be protected from dangerous animals such as tigers, leopards, wolves, elephants, and
lions. Pure quartz is also an amulet giving the wearer extraordinary sexual prowess. Wearing
quartz while offering libations to departed ancestors insures them lasting happiness. It is also a
talisman against drowning, burning and theft. These attributes pertain to pure flawless quartz,
and knowledgeable gemologists advise that flawed varieties that are included, fractured, or
discolored should be completely avoided.

Bloodstone

Similar to a bloodstone, flawless coral constitutes the perfect Mars Astral Talisman. Flawless red coral handcrafted in 18k gold. Piece no.159

Vedic Text

The complexion of *Vala* was taken by the demigod of fire, *Agnideva*. It transformed into the seed-origin of bloodstone and dropped primarily into India's Narmada River. Some of these seeds washed upon the lands occupied by the lower caste populace while the rest spread around India and other parts of the world. Wherever they settled, deposits of bloodstone originated.

Bloodstones of good quality are colored green with reddish spots, and can be highly polished because of their density. Exceptionally fine bloodstones are occasionally found with colors which radiate as brightly as lightning. Bloodstones of fine quality increase the wealth and followers of one who wears them.

Throughout these ancient texts. The importance of both purity & color as the root source of cosmic power in gems is always emphasized. Gems free of defects are regarded as pure transmitters of astral energy and are therefore auspicious. Flawed gems, on the other hand, have just the opposite affect - they were seen to attract ill-fortune. Nowadays clarity and quality are simply factors which affect the price of gems.

In the following chapter we list the gemologial data currently used by modern-day gemologists to identify unknown gemstones and to separate natural gems from their synthetic counterparts.

The creation of matter was a subject analyzed in ancient vedic texts and narratives of art for thousands of years.......

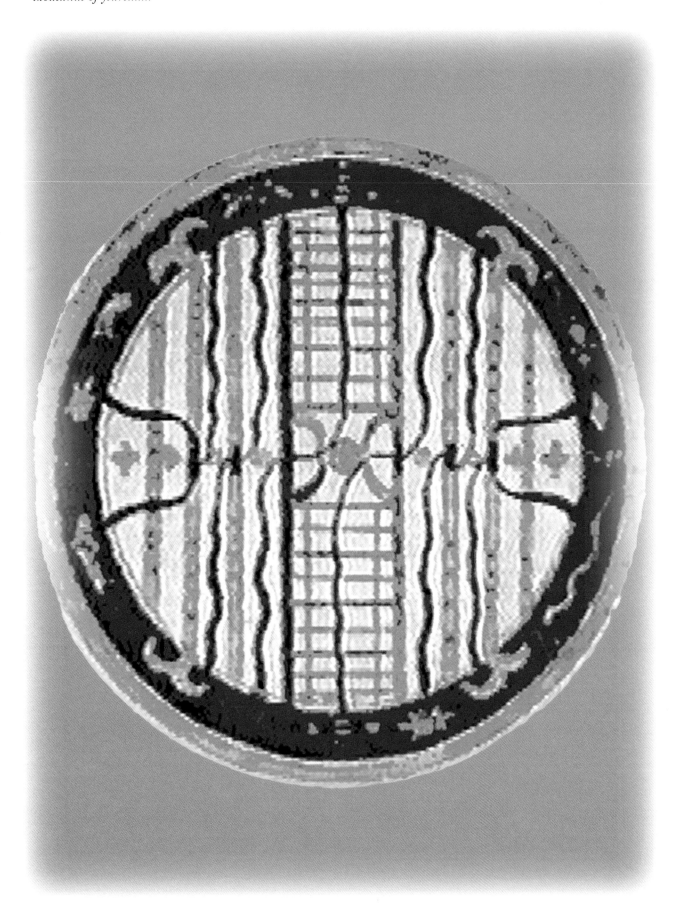

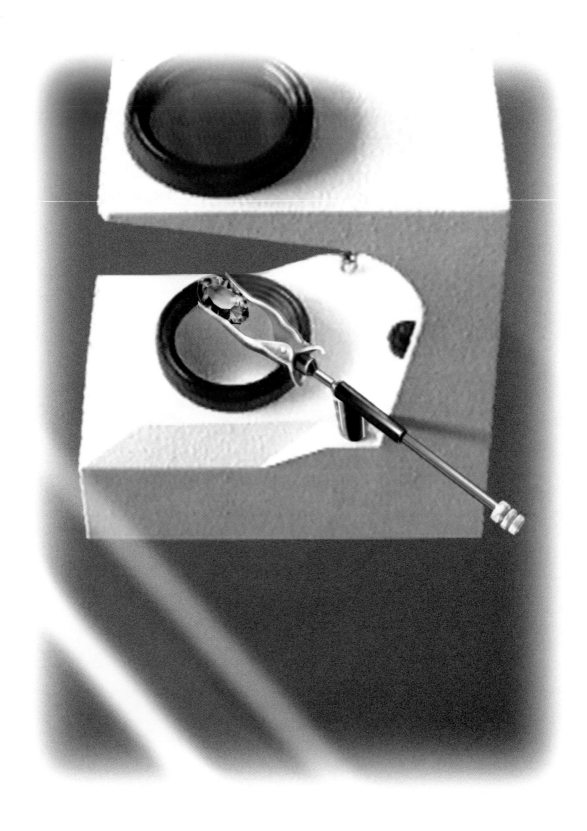

Modern polariscope for testing gemstones for single or double refraction. Some elements of this instrument are polarizing filters

VIII

Modern Gemological Data

"Ruby, emerald, blue sapphire, cat's eye, yellow sapphire, diamond, pearl, hessonite, coral, bloodstone, quartz, jade, and red garnet are the foremost species of gems, and they should be selected only under the expert guidance of a learned gemologist."

Sri Garuda-puranam (Circa 2,500 BC)

THE basic gemological characteristics of the principal gemstones used in astral gem therapy are listed below. These factors are used by gemologists throughout the world today to scientifically identify and grade the quality of precious gems. Combined with the astrological attributes of gems discussed in the foregoing chapters, this gemological information gives a complete picture of the nature of each gemstone. Gems are listed according to the planet with which each type of stone is astrologically associated, beginning with the Sun. Present sources and other information will be limited to those sources and characteristics which pertain to 'gem' (auspicious) quality only.

◆————————————

Gemstones of the Sun

1. Ruby

Present Sources: Burma, Thailand, Sri Lanka, Cambodia, Laos & Vietnam

Gemological Characteristics:

SPECIES:	corundum
TRANSPARENCY:	transparent
COLOR:	red, orangish-red, violetish-red, purplish-red, pinkish-red, pink & blackish-red.
REFRACTIVE INDEX:	1.763 – 1.770
BIREFRINGENCE:	0.008
PLEOCHROISM:	strong dichroism
CRYSTAL SYSTEM:	hexagonal
OPTIC CHARACTER:	doubly refractive
SPECIFIC GRAVITY:	4.00
MOHS HARDNESS:	9
DISPERSION:	0.018
FLUORESCENCE:	long wave – weak to strong red
IDENTIFYING VISUAL CHARACTERISTICS:	fingerprint inclusions, hexagonal growth lines, silk (rutile) and straight color banding.

2. Red Spinel

Present Sources: Sri Lanka, Burma and Thailand

Gemological Characteristics

SPECIES:	spinel
TRANSPARENCY:	transparent
COLOR:	red, pink-red, pink, purple-red, violet red, orange-brownish red
REFRACTIVE INDEX:	1.718
CRYSTAL SYSTEM:	cubic
OPTIC CHARACTER:	singly refractive
SPECIFIC GRAVITY:	3.6
MOHS HARDNESS:	8
DISPERSION:	0.02
FLUORESCENCE:	long wave – weak to strong red-orange, short wave – inert to weak red.
IDENTIFYING VISUAL CHARACTERISTICS:	natural inclusions, e.g. needles, fingerprint inclusions of spinel octahedra, etc.

Flawless Sun jewel. handcrafted in 18k gold. Piece no.989

3. Red Garnet

Present Sources:

Almandite: Burma, India, Sri Lank, Brazil, Western U.S.A. and many other areas around the world.
Rhodolite: Sri Lanka, U.S.A., and E. Africa.
Pyrope: U.S.A., Czechoslovakia, Australia, South Africa, Brazil, Sri Lanka and Madagascar

Gemological Characteristics

SPECIES (1):	almandite
TRANSPARENCY:	transparent
COLOR:	violetish-red to brownish-red
REFRACTIVE INDEX:	1.79
CRYSTAL SYSTEM:	cubic
OPTIC CHARACTER:	singly refractive
SPECIFIC GRAVITY:	4.05
MOHS HARDNESS:	7.5
DISPERSION:	0.024
IDENTIFYING VISUAL CHARACTERISTICS:	needlelike inclusions frequently intersecting at 70° and 110° in same plane, coarse stubby silk, and doubly refractive colorless grain-like inclusions.

SPECIES(2):	rhodolite
TRANSPARENCY:	transparent
COLOR:	red to violet-red
REFRACTIVE INDEX:	1.76
CRYSTAL SYSTEM:	cubic
OPTIC CHARACTER:	singly refractive
SPECIFIC GRAVITY:	3.84
MOHS HARDNESS:	7 – 7.5
DISPERSION:	0.026
INDENTIFYING VISUAL CHARACTERISTICS:	same as almandite (typical garnet inclusions); purplish-red color and variable refractive index of 1.75 – 1.77 possible.

SPECIES(3):	pyrope
TRANSPARENCY:	transparent
COLOR:	brownish red
REFRACTIVE INDEX:	1.746
CRYSTAL SYSTEM:	cubic
OPTIC CHARACTER:	singly refractive
SPECIFIC GRAVITY:	3.78
MOHS HARDNESS:	7 – 7.5
DISPERSION:	0.027
IDENTIFYING VISUAL CHARACTERISTICS:	typical garnet inclusions, same as almandite.

4. Rubellite

Present Sources: Sri Lanka, Burma, South West Africa, Ural Mountains (Russia), Brazil, Madagascar, Maine and California (USA).

Gemological Characteristics

SPECIES:	tourmaline
TRANSPARENCY:	transparent
COLOR:	pink to red
REFRACTIVE INDEX:	1.62 – 1.64
BIREFRINGENCE:	0.02
PLEOCHROISM:	strong dichroism
CRYSTAL SYSTEM:	hexagonal
OPTIC CHARACTER:	doubly refractive
SPECIFIC GRAVITY:	3.06
MOHS HARDNESS:	7 – 7.5
DISPERSION:	0.017
FLUORESCENCE:	not significant
IDENTIFYING VISUAL CHARACTERISTICS:	color zoning, natural inclusions, e.g. threadlike gas inclusions, and moderate doubling of back facets.

1. Pearl

Present Sources: Natural Oyster Pearl – Persian Gulf (Bahrain), Sri Lanka, Venezuela, Bengal, Bombay, Australia and the South Pacific.

Gemological Characteristics:

SPECIES:	natural pearl
TRANSPARENCY:	translucent to opaque
COLOR:	white, pink rose, cream, yellowish, greenish, blue, gray and black.
REFRACTIVE INDEX:	1.530 – 1.686
CRYSTAL SYSTEM:	aggregate
SPECIFIC GRAVITY:	2.7
MOHS HARDNESS:	2.5 – 4.5
FLUORESCENCE:	long wave – inert to strong, short wave – inert to moderate.
IDENTIFYING VISUAL CHARACTERISTICS:	orient, gritty texture when rubbed on teeth, best test to separate natural from cultured is X-radiograph.

2. Moonstone

Present Sources: Sri Lanka, Burma, Central and Southern India.

Gemological Characteristics:

SPECIES:	orthoclase feldspar
TRANSPARENCY:	transparent to translucent
COLOR:	colorless and white with white/bluish adularescence
REFRACTIVE INDEX:	1.518 – 1.526
BIREFRINGENCE:	0.008
PLEOCHROISM:	weak dichorism
CRYSTAL SYSTEM:	monoclinic
OPTIC CHARACTER:	doubly refractive
SPECIFIC GRAVITY:	2.56
MOHS HARDNESS:	6 – 6.5
DISPERSION:	0.012
FLUORESCENCE:	not significant
IDENTIFYING VISUAL CHARACTERISTICS:	adularescence (floating white-bluish light), near perfect cleavage, splintery uneven fracture, 'centipede' inclusions.

1. Yellow Sapphire

Present Sources: Sri Lanka, Thailand, Burma and Cambodia.

Gemological Characteristics

SPECIES:	corundum
TRANSPARENCY:	transparent
COLOR:	light-yellow, yellow, golden-yellow, brownish yellow, golden, orangish-yellow, golden-orange, and pinkish-orange (*padparadscha*)
REFRACTIVE INDEX:	1.762 – 1.770
BIREFRINGENCE:	0.008
PLEOCHROISM:	strong dichroism
CRYSTAL SYSTEM:	hexagonal
OPTIC CHARACTER:	doubly refractive
SPECIFIC GRAVITY:	4
MOHS HARDNESS:	9
DISPERSION:	0.018
FLUORESCENCE:	colorless sapphire – inert to strong reddish (long wave), – inert to moderate orange (short wave)
IDENTIFYING VISUAL CHARACTERISTICS:	fingerprint inclusions, hexagonal growth lines, silk (rutile), straight color-banding

*Jupiter Astral Talisman.
Flawless yellow sapphire
handcrafted in 18k
yellow gold.
Piece no.148*

2. Yellow Topaz

Present Sources Brazil, Sri Lanka, Africa, Mexico and U.S.A.

Gemological Characteristics

SPECIES :	topaz
TRANSPARENCY :	transparent
COLOR :	yellow, golden, sherry, pinkish-yellow, yellow-brown, brownish-orange
REFRACTIVE INDEX :	1.619 – 1.627
BIREFRINGENCE :	0.008
PLEOCHROISM :	weak to strong dichroism and trichroism
CRYSTAL SYSTEM :	orthorhombic
OPTIC CHARACTER :	doubly refractive
SPECIFIC GRAVITY :	3.52
MOHS HARDNESS :	8
DISPERSION:	0.014
FLUORESCENCE :	long wave – inert to weak yellow
IDENTIFYING VISUAL CHARACTERISTICS :	liquid, gas and other natural inclusions, basel cleavage, possible 3-phase inclusions, and 'rhombic' (four sided) etch markings.

3. Citrine

Present Sources Brazil, Madagascar, Uruguay, and many other minor sources throughout the world.

Gemological Characteristics

SPECIES :	quartz
TRANSPARENCY :	transparent
COLOR :	yellow, golden, orangish yellow, and brownish yellow
REFRACTIVE INDEX :	1.544 – 1.553
BIREFRINGENCE :	0.009
PLEOCHROISM :	weak to strong dichroism
CRYSTAL SYSTEM :	hexagonal
OPTIC CHARACTER :	doubly refractive
SPECIFIC GRAVITY :	2.66
MOHS HARDNESS :	7
DISPERSION :	0.013
FLUORESCENCE :	not significant
IDENTIFYING VISUAL CHARACTERISTICS :	vitreous conchoidal fracture, liquid inclusions, 2-phase inclusions, negative crystals, color zoning or banding, and uneven coloration.

4. Heliodor

Present Sources: Brazil, Russia (Sverdlovsk), Madagascar, U.S.A. (S.California), South Africa, and a few other areas around the world.

Gemological Characteristics:

SPECIES :	beryl
TRANSPARENCY :	transparent
COLOR :	light to golden yellow
REFRACTIVE INDEX :	1.577 – 1.583
BIREFRINGENCE :	0.005 – 0.009
PLEOCHROISM :	weak greenish yellow, and yellow
CRYSTAL SYSTEM :	hexagonal
OPTIC CHARACTER :	doubly refractive
SPECIFIC GRAVITY :	2.67 – 2.84
MOHS HARDNESS :	7.5
DISPERSION :	0.014
FLUORESCENCE :	none
IDENTIFYING VISUAL CHARACTERISTICS :	typical 3 phase and 2 phase inclusions, inclusions of calcite, pyrite, mica and/or tremolite needles, etc.

◆ *Gemstones of Rahu*

1. Hessonite

Rahu Astral Talisman. Flawless hessonite handcrafted in 18k gold. Piece no.66

Present Sources: Sri Lanka, Africa, India and Burma.

Gemological Characteristics:

SPECIES :	grossularite
TRANSPARENCY :	transparent
COLOR :	golden orange, brownish orange and reddish orange
REFRACTIVE INDEX :	1.74 – 1.75
CRYSTAL SYSTEM :	cubic
OPTIC CHARACTER :	singly refractive
SPECIFIC GRAVITY :	3.61
MOHS HARDNESS :	7
DISPERSION :	0.028
FLUORESCENCE :	inert
IDENTIFYING VISUAL CHARACTERISTICS :	roiled (heat-wave) internal appearance, garnet inclusions, anomalous double refraction and strain colors may be visible in polariscope.

2. Orange Zircon

Present Sources: Burma, Sri Lanka, Thailand and Viet Nam
Gemological Characteristics:

SPECIES :	zircon
TRANSPARENCY :	transparent
COLOR :	yellow-orange, orange, orange-red, reddish-brown, and brown
REFRACTIVE INDEX :	1.875 (medium), 1.925 – 1.984 (high),
BIREFRINGENCE :	0.006 – .050 (medium), 0.059 (high)
PLEOCHROISM :	weak to strong dichroism
CRYSTAL SYSTEM :	tetragonal
OPTIC CHARACTER :	doubly refractive
SPECIFIC GRAVITY :	4.32 (medium), 4.70 (high)
MOHS HARDNESS :	7.5
DISPERSION :	0.038
FLUORESCENCE :	short wave-inert to strong orange and/or inert to strong yellow, long wave-inert to moderate yellow
IDENTIFYING VISUAL CHARACTERISTICS :	strong doubling of back facet junctions, abraded facet edges, sub-admantine luster, natural inclusions.

3. Spessartite

Present Sources: Sri Lanka, Burma, Madagascar, Brazil, Australia, and U.S.A.
Gemological Characteristics:

SPECIES:	spessartite
TRANSPARENCY:	transparent
COLOR:	golden orange to orangish-red
REFRACTIVE INDEX:	1.810
CRYSTAL SYSTEM:	cubic
OPTIC CHARACTER:	singly refractive
SPECIFIC GRAVITY:	4.15
MOHS HARDNESS:	7 – 7.5
DISPERSION:	0.027
IDENTIFYING VISUAL CHARACTERISTICS:	needlelike inclusions frequently intersecting at 70° and 110° in same plane, coarse stubby silk, and doubly refractive colorless grain-like inclusions.

*Mercury & Venus Astral
Talisman. Flawless
diopside and diamond
handcrafted in 21k gold.
Piece no.170*

1. Emerald

Present Sources: South America (primarily Columbia and Brazil), Africa (Sandewana, Kenya, Tanzania, Zambia, Mozambique), India, Pakistan, Russia (Ural Mountains), and Egypt

Gemological Characteristics:

SPECIES :	beryl
TRANSPARENCY :	transparent
COLOR :	green, yellowish-green and bluish green
REFRACTIVE INDEX :	1.577 – 1.583
BIREFRINGENCE :	0.005 – 0.009
PLEOCHROISM :	weak to strong dichroism
CRYSTAL SYSTEM :	hexagonal
OPTIC CHARACTER :	doubly refractive
SPECIFIC GRAVITY :	2.72
MOHS HARDNESS :	7.5 – 8
DISPERSION :	0.014
FLUORESCENCE :	inert to weak green (long and short wave)
IDENTIFYING VISUAL CHARACTERISTICS :	typical 3 phase and 2 phase inclusions, inclusions of calcite, pyrite, mica and/or tremolite needles, etc.

2. Green Jade

Present Sources: Jadeite – Burma; Nephrite – China, New Zealand and U.S.A.

Gemological Characteristics:

SPECIES (1) :	jadeite
TRANSPARENCY :	transluent
COLOR :	intense green to mottled green
REFRACTIVE INDEX :	1.660 – 1.668 (1.66)
CRYSTAL SYSTEM :	monoclinic (aggregate)
SPECIFIC GRAVITY :	3.34
MOHS HARDNESS :	6.5 – 7
IDENTIFYING VISUAL CHARACTERISTICS :	greasy to waxy luster, spectroscopic reading of 4370 at the edge of the violet is conclusive identity of translucent, light-colored jadeite.

SPECIES (2) :   nephrite
TRANSPARENCY :   translucent
COLOR :   dark green
REFRACTIVE INDEX :   1.61 – 1.63 (1.61)
CRYSTAL SYSTEM :   monoclinic (aggregate)
SPECIFIC GRAVITY :   2.95
MOHS HARDNESS :   6 – 6.5
IDENTIFYING VISUAL
CHARACTERISTICS :   rough fracture with dull luster.
                                        Black inclusions may be visible.

3. Peridot

Present Sources: Burma, Zebirget Island (Red Sea), Arizona (USA).
Gemological Characteristics:

SPECIES :   peridot
TRANSPARENCY: tranparent
COLOR :   green, yellow-green, brownish-green
REFRACTIVE INDEX :   1.654 – 1.690
BIREFRINGENCE :   0.036
PLEOCHROISM :   weak dichroism
CRYSTAL SYSTEM :   orthorhombic
OPTIC CHARACTER :   doubly refractive
SPECIFIC GRAVITY :   3.34
MOHS HARDNESS :   6.5 – 7
DISPERSION :   0.020
FLUORESCENCE :   not significant
IDENTIFYING VISUAL
CHARACTERISTICS :   vitreous conchoidal fracture, strong
                                        doubling of back facets, natural inclusions,
                                        e.g. lily pad, black chromite crystals
                                        and iron oxide inclusions.

Mercury Astral Talisman.
Flawless tourmaline
& herb-cache handcrafted
in 21k gold.
Piece no.757

4. Green Tourmaline

Present Sources: Sri Lanka, Burma, South West Africa, Ural Mountains (Russia), Brazil, Madagascar, Maine and California (USA)

Gemological Characteristics:

SPECIES :	tourmaline
TRANSPARENCY :	transparent
COLOR :	chrome-green, yellow-green, blue-green and brownish-green
REFRACTIVE INDEX :	1.62 – 1.64
BIREFRINGENCE :	0.020
PLEOCHROISM :	strong dichroism
CRYSTAL SYSTEM :	hexagonal
OPTIC CHARACTER :	doubly refractive
SPECIFIC GRAVITY :	3.06
MOHS HARDNESS :	7 – 7.5
DISPERSION :	0.017
FLUORESCENCE :	not significant
IDENTIFYING VISUAL CHARACTERISTICS :	color zoning, natural inclusions, e.g. threadlike liquid and gas inclusions, and moderate doubling of back facets.

5. Tsavorite

Present Sources   Kenya and Tanzania in Africa

Gemological Characteristics

SPECIES :	grossularite
TRANSPARENCY :	transparent
COLOR :	chrome green
REFRACTIVE INDEX :	1.73 – 1.75
CRYSTAL SYSTEM :	cubic
OPTIC CHARACTER :	singly refractive
SPECIFIC GRAVITY :	3.61 (3.30 – 4.30)
MOHS HARDNESS :	7 - 7.25
DISPERSION :	0.028
FLUORESCENCE :	long and short wave – inert to red
IDENTIFYING VISUAL CHARACTERISTICS :	stubby, rounded, included crystals of low relief, occasional needles, fractures and bubbly veils.

6. Green Diopside

Present Sources: Brazil, Sri Lanka, Italy and USA.

Gemological Characteristics:

SPECIES :	diopside
TRANSPARENCY :	transparent
COLOR :	chrome green (recommended color)
REFRACTIVE INDEX :	1.675 – 1.701
BIREFRINGENCE :	0.026
PLEOCHROISM :	weak dichroism and trichroism
CRYSTAL SYSTEM :	monoclinic
OPTIC CHARACTER :	doubly refractive
SPECIFIC GRAVITY :	3.26 – 3.32
MOHS HARDNESS :	5 – 6
IDENTIFYING VISUAL CHARACTERISTICS :	confused with peridot but with lower birefringence and higher refractive index.

*Mercury Astral Talisman.
Flawless tourmaline, handcrafted with herb caches in 18k gold.
Piece no.341*

1. Diamond

Present Sources: Africa (Botswana, Tanzania, Sierra Leone, Angola, Republic of Liberia and Ivory Coast), Brazil, Venezuela, Guyana, Indonesia, India, Russia and Australia.

Gemological Characteristics:

SPECIES :	diamond
TRANSPARENCY :	transparent
COLOR :	colorless to tints of yellow, brown, blue, pink, chartreuse and black
REFRACTIVE INDEX :	2.417
CRYSTAL SYSTEM :	cubic
OPTIC CHARACTER :	singly refractive
SPECIFIC GRAVITY :	3.52
MOHS HARDNESS :	10
DISPERSION :	0.044
FLUORESCENCE :	inert to very strong bluish-white (long and short wave)
IDENTIFYING VISUAL CHARACTERISTICS :	adamantine luster, naturals, waxy to rough girdle surface, sharpness of facet edges, reflectivity meter of diamond probe helps separate diamonds from substitutes.

2. Rock Crystal

Present Sources: Nepal, India, Pakistan, Brazil and practically every country in the world.

Gemological Characteristics:

SPECIES :	quartz
TRANSPARENCY :	transparent
COLOR :	white (colorless)
REFRACTIVE INDEX :	1.544 – 1.553
BIREFRINGENCE :	0.009
CRYSTAL SYSTEM :	hexagonal
OPTIC CHARACTER :	doubly refractive
SPECIFIC GRAVITY :	2.66
MOHS HARDNESS :	7
DISPERSION :	0.013
FLUORESCENCE :	nil
IDENTIFYING VISUAL CHARACTERISTICS :	conchoidal fracture with vitreous luster on fracture surface, negative liquid and crystal inclusions.

3. White Zircon

Present Sources: Sri Lanka, Burma, Thailand and Vietnam

Gemological Characteristics:

SPECIES :	zircon
TRANSPARENCY :	transparent
COLOR :	colorless
REFRACTIVE INDEX :	1.875 – 1.905 (medium),
	1.925 – 1.984 (high)
PLEOCHROISM :	weak to strong dichroism
CRYSTAL SYSTEM :	tetragonal
OPTIC CHARACTER :	doubly refractive
SPECIFIC GRAVITY :	4.32 (medium), 4.70 (high)
MOHS HARDNESS :	7.5
DISPERSION :	0.038
FLUORESCENCE :	not significant
IDENTIFYING VISUAL CHARACTERISTICS :	natural angular inclusions, abraded facet junctions, strong doubling of back facets.

4. Goshenite

Present Sources: Sri Lanka, Brazil, Madagascar, Russia, California and Maine.

Gemological Characteristics:

SPECIES :	beryl
TRANSPARENCY :	transparent
COLOR :	white (colorless)
REFRACTIVE INDEX :	1.577 – 1.583 (generally low)
BIREFRINGENCE :	0.005 – 0.009 (generally low)
PLEOCHROISM :	weak dichroism
CRYSTAL SYSTEM :	hexagonal
OPTIC CHARACTER :	doubly refractive
SPECIFIC GRAVITY :	2.72
MOHS HARDNESS :	7.5
DISPERSION :	0.014
FLUORESCENCE :	not significant
IDENTIFYING VISUAL CHARACTERISTICS :	fiberous inclusions, parallel tubes, fingerprint pattern (liquid filled) inclusions and 2-phase (liquid and gas) inclusions.

Venus Astral Talisman. Flawless diamond handcrafted in 18k gold. Piece no.1064

5. White Topaz

Present Sources: Brazil, Sri Lanka, Africa, Mexico and U.S.A.

Gemological Characteristics:

SPECIES :	topaz
TRANSPARENCY :	transparent
COLOR :	white (colorless)
REFRACTIVE INDEX :	1.619 – 1.627
BIREFRINGENCE :	0.008
CRYSTAL SYSTEM :	orthorhombic
OPTIC CHARACTER :	doubly refractive
SPECIFIC GRAVITY :	3.52
MOHS HARDNESS :	0.014
FLUORESCENCE :	long wave – inert to weak yellow, to pink
IDENTIFYING VISUAL CHARACTERISTICS :	liquid, gas and other natural inclusions, basel cleavage, possible 3-phase inclusions, and 'rhombic' (four sided) etch markings

◆───────────

Gemstones of Ketu

1. Cat's Eye

Present Sources   Sri Lanka, Brazil, South India, and Burma.

Gemological Characteristics

SPECIES :	chrysoberyl
TRANSPARENCY :	transparent to translucent
COLOR :	yellow, greenish-yellow, brownish-yellow,
REFRACTIVE INDEX :	1.746 – 1.755
BIREFRINGENCE :	0.009
PLEOCHROISM :	weak to strong dichroism to trichroism
CRYSTAL SYSTEM :	orthorhombic
OPTIC CHARACTER :	doubly refractive
SPECIFIC GRAVITY :	3.73
MOHS HARDNESS :	8.50
DISPERSION :	0.015
FLUORESCENCE :	nil
IDENTIFYING VISUAL CHARACTERISTICS :	strong chatoyant 'cat's eye' looking light band caused by minute light reflection on included crystal fibers or tubes, also natural and fingerprint inclusions.

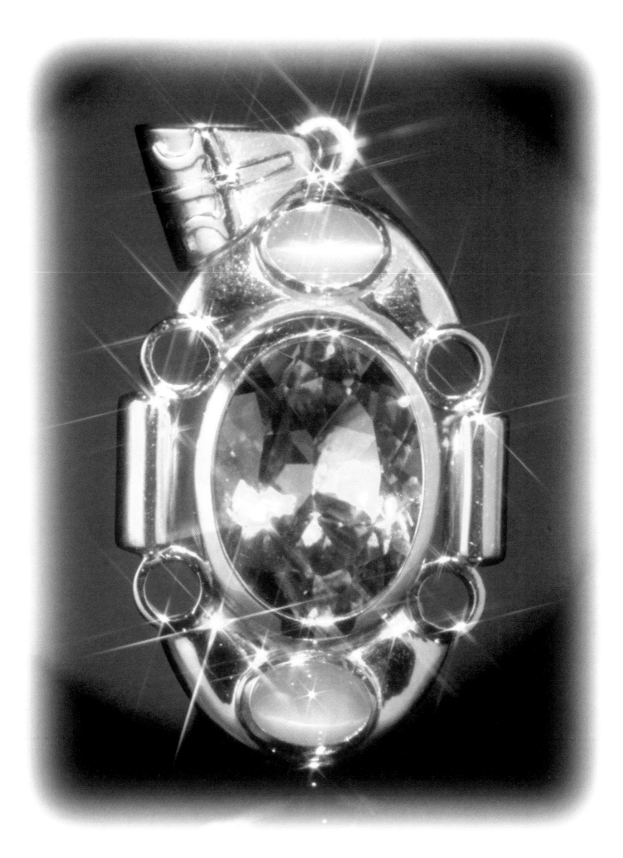

Ketu Astral Talisman.
Flawless cat's eyes
and yellow beryl
handcrafted in 21k
gold. Piece no.450

2. Apatite Cat's Eye

Present Sources: Sri Lanka, Burma, Bohemia, Mexico, Maine (USA), and other sources.

Gemological Characteristics:

SPECIES :	apatite
TRANSPARENCY :	transparent to translucent
COLOR :	yellow, yellow-green, green, gray-green, brownish green-yellow
REFRACTIVE INDEX :	1.642 - 1.646
BIREFRINGENCE :	.002 - .006
PLEOCHROISM :	weak to strong dichroism
CRYSTAL SYSTEM :	hexagonal
OPTIC CHARACTER :	doubly refractive
SPECIFIC GRAVITY :	3.18
MOHS HARDNESS :	5
DISPERSION :	0.013
FLUORESCENCE :	long wave – moderate yellowish to dark greenish, short wave – weak yellowish to dark greenish; long and short wave – inert to moderate light pinkish
IDENTIFYING VISUAL CHARACTERISTICS :	similar to chrysoberyl and tourmaline cat's eyes except for lower properties.

3. Tourmaline Cat's Eye

Present Sources: Sri Lanka, Burma, South West Africa, Ural Mountains (Russia), Brazil, Madagascar, Maine and California (USA).

Gemological Characteristics:

SPECIES :	tourmaline
TRANSPARENCY :	transparent to translucent
COLOR :	chrome-green, yellow-green, blue-green, brownish-green
REFRACTIVE INDEX :	1.62 – 1.64
BIREFRINGENCE :	0.020
PLEOCHROISM :	strong dichroism
CRYSTAL SYSTEM :	hexagonal
OPTIC CHARACTER :	doubly refractive
SPECIFIC GRAVITY :	3.06
MOHS HARDNESS :	7 –7.5
DISPERSION :	0.017
FLUORESCENCE :	not significant
IDENTIFYING VISUAL CHARACTERISTICS :	color zoning, natural inclusions, e.g. threadlike liquid and gas inclusions, with chatoyant 'cat's eye' effect.

1. Blue Sapphire

Present Sources: Burma, Sri Lanka, Thailand & Cambodia.
Gemological Characteristics:

SPECIES :	corundum
TRANSPARENCY :	transparent
COLOR :	blue, violetish-blue, greenish-blue, blackish-blue, gray blue, purple and violet
REFRACTIVE INDEX :	1.762 – 1.770
BIREFRINGENCE :	0.008
PLEOCHROISM :	strong dichroism
CRYSTAL SYSTEM :	hexagonal
OPTIC CHARACTER :	doubly refractive
SPECIFIC GRAVITY :	4
MOHS HARDNESS :	9
DISPERSION :	0.018
FLUORESCENCE :	light blue sapphire – moderate to strong pink (long wave), purple and violet sapphire – inert to strong reddish violet (long wave) and inert to moderate reddish (short wave)
IDENTIFYING VISUAL CHARACTERISTICS :	fingerprint inclusions, hexagonal growth lines, silk (rutile) and straight color banding.

2. Tanzanite

Present Sources: Tanzania (Africa).
Gemological Characteristics:

SPECIES :	zoisite
TRANSPARENCY :	transparent
COLOR :	blue, violetish-blue
REFRACTIVE INDEX :	1.691 – 1.704
BIREFRINGENCE :	0.013
PLEOCHROISM :	weak to strong dichroism
CRYSTAL SYSTEM :	orthorhombic
OPTIC CHARACTER :	doubly refractive
SPECIFIC GRAVITY :	3.30
MOHS HARDNESS :	6 – 7
DISPERSION :	0.021
FLUORESCENCE :	not significant
IDENTIFYING VISUAL CHARACTERISTICS :	strong blue and violet pleochroism.
NOTE:	As tanzanite is usually heat-enhanced we do not whole-heartedly recommend it for astrological use.

3. Blue Spinel

Present Sources: Burma, Thailand and Sri Lanka.

Gemological Characteristics:

SPECIES :	spinel
TRANSPARENCY :	transparent
COLOR:	blue, violet-blue and purplish-blue
REFRACTIVE INDEX :	1.718
CRYSTAL SYSTEM :	cubic
OPTIC CHARACTER :	singly refractive
SPECIFIC GRAVITY :	3.60
MOHS HARDNESS :	8
DISPERSION :	0.020
FLUORESCENCE :	not significant
IDENTIFYING VISUAL CHARACTERISTICS :	natural inclusions, e.g., needles, spinel octahedral crystals (often in fingerprint pattern), and iron oxide inclusions

4. Amethyst

Present Sources: Brazil, Ural Mountains (Russia), Uruguay, Arizona (USA) and to some extent in almost every part of the world.

Gemological Characteristics:

SPECIES :	quartz
TRANSPARENCY :	transparent
COLOR :	purple
REFRACTIVE INDEX :	1.544 – 1.553
BIREFRINGENCE :	0.009
PLEOCHROISM :	weak to strong dichroism
CRYSTAL SYSTEM :	hexagonal
OPTIC CHARACTER :	doubly refractive
SPECIFIC GRAVITY :	2.66
MOHS HARDNESS :	7
DISPERSION :	0.013
FLUORESCENCE :	not significant
IDENTIFYING VISUAL CHARACTERISTICS :	vitreous conchoidal fracture, liquid inclusions, 2-phase inclusions, negative crystals, color zoning or banding, and uneven coloration.

1. Coral

Present Sources: Mediterranean Sea, Red Sea, Persian Gulf, and the coasts of Algeria, Tunisia, Taiwan, Spain, Italy, Japan and Australia.

Gemological Characteristics:

SPECIES :	coral
TRANSPARENCY :	translucent
COLOR :	red, pink, reddish-orange and orange
REFRACTIVE INDEX :	1.486 – 1.658
CRYSTAL SYSTEM :	aggregate
SPECIFIC GRAVITY :	2.65
MOHS HARDNESS :	3.5 - 4
DISPERSION :	0.038
IDENTIFYING VISUAL CHARACTERISTICS :	wavy parallel fibrous structure, uneven fracture with dull luster.

2. Carnelian

Present Sources: Brazil, India, Uruguay and many other places.

Gemological Characteristics:

SPECIES :	chalcedony
TRANSPARENCY :	semi-translucent
COLOR:	red, orange-red, brownish-red, or brownish-orange
REFRACTIVE INDEX :	1.535 – 1.539
CRYSTAL SYSTEM :	hexagonal
OPTIC CHARACTER :	aggregate
SPECIFIC GRAVITY :	2.60
MOHS HARDNESS :	6.5 -7
FLUORESCENCE :	not significant
IDENTIFYING VISUAL CHARACTERISTICS :	dull to waxy conchoidal fracture.

Mars Astral Talisman. Flawless coral & herb tube set in 21k gold. Piece no.367

Moon Astral Talisman.
Flawless moonstone, red spinels &
herb caches set in 18k gold.
Piece no.571

3. Bloodstone

Present Sources: Brazil, India, uruguay and many other places.

Gemological Characteristics:

SPECIES :	chalcedony
TRANSPARENCY :	opaque
COLOR :	red, orange-red, brownish-red, or brownish-green
REFRACTIVE INDEX :	1.535 – 1.539
CRYSTAL SYSTEM :	hexagonal
OPTIC CHARACTER :	aggregate
SPECIFIC GRAVITY :	2.60
MOHS HARDNESS :	6.5 – 7
FLUORESCENCE :	not significant
IDENTIFYING VISUAL CHARACTERISTICS :	conchoidal fracture with dull to luster on the fracture surface, distinguishing it from glass. There are no substitutes which imitate bloodstone closely.

With all the above information at hand, anyone can determine which sort of gemstone best suits his or her astrological requirements, then refer to the scientific gemological data for proper identification of the gemstone(s) of choice. When choosing gems for astro-therapy, it is always best to first consult a qualified sidereal astrologer in order to correctly cast one's individual horoscope according to the ancient but highly accurate *Vedic* system of India. And when purchasing astrologically potent gems, one should deal exclusively with reputable suppliers and be prepared to pay (in some cases) fairly steep prices. Only flawless gems transmit positive energies from the planets to the wearer, and **flawless** gems are usually rare and can be expensive. It's far better to wear no gems at all than to wear flawed, inexpensive ones, because inferior specimens not only fail to transmit positive energies, they actually attract negative influences

On the following pages let us give you some insights to the fascinating world of Astral Gem-stone Talismans, where, with the aid of modern technology, the aspirant to cosmic analysis will find expert assistance in the quest for his or her perfect astrological gem & setting.

Early interchange of
Western and Eastern
scientific thought: an
astrolabe for the calculation
of astronomical (and
therefore also astrological)
relationships. Crafted in
Western India in the
18th century

IX

The Creation of Modern Astrological Gemstone Talismans

An Astral Gemstone Talisman is a ring, a pendant, earrings or a bangle, uniquely crafted in either 18k or 21k gold. Each piece is a singular work of art adorned with clean, exceptional (auspicious) jewels of the highest quality.

Astral Gemstone Talismans are created to suit your specific requirements according to a detailed 'astrological prescription'. Based upon this prescription, AGT will provide your own personal piece. Astral Gemstone Talismans are designed according to a unique concept from ancient *Vedic* texts.

Each Talisman is numbered and stamped with the designer's personal seal and comes with its own Certificate of Authenticity and Description of Astral Aspects and Influences.

Unique, personalized, and completely original, each Astral Gemstone Talisman is a genuine collector's item that also provides benefits which money cannot buy.

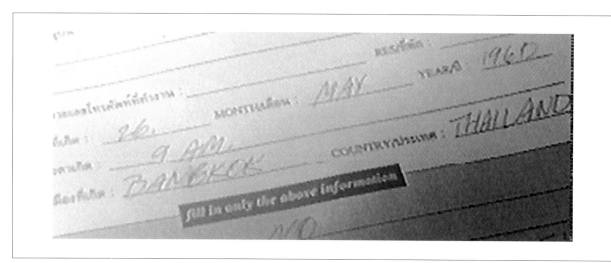

The customer provides his or her birthday, hour and location of birth in a standard form

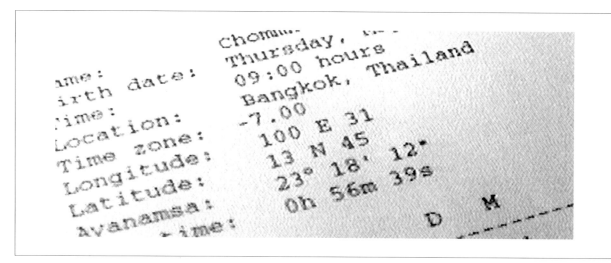

Trained attendants check for additional details, such as day-light savings time in force at the place of birth at the time, and adjust the data accordingly

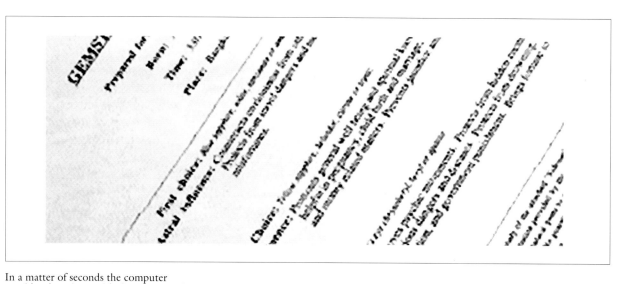

In a matter of seconds the computer provides the printer with the answers. The positions of constellations at the time of birth, their effects on the client's karma, and the recommended gemstone(s) for a most auspicous future are printed, and bound into an attractive folder

Details of the position of the planets at the time of birth

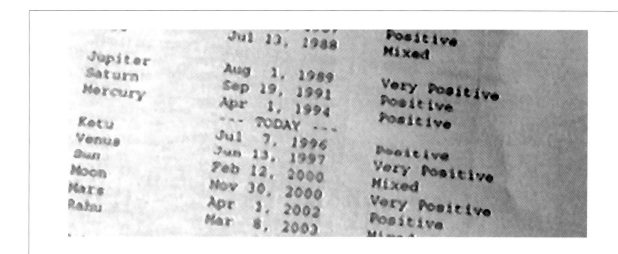

The effect of the planetary periods on the Karma of the client from birth well into the 21st century

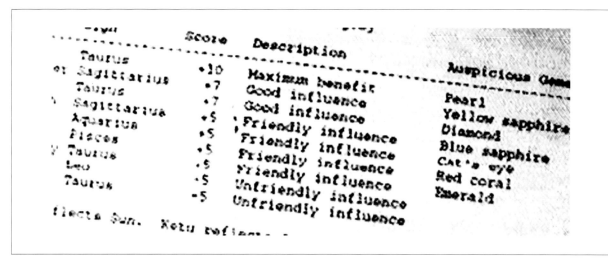

The most recommended gemstone(s) for an enhanced Karma, as well as planets of negative influence to the individual

In the meantime gem merchants in suits
or dhotis search the globe for the perfect
gem.....

... and finally bring them to Thailand where
they are carefully selected for color and
clarity

The task is difficult; as shrinking resources of
quality gems drive up their prices
relentlessly. Only perfect stones are kept in
the vaults of AGT

Every year AGT orders ashes of sacred,
auspicious plants directly from Nepal

Sorted for their benign, complementary
influence on specific categories of gems they
are guarded until their use in AGT jewelry

They are filled into tiny golden tubes that
form permanent companions to many gems
used in AGT designs

Mercury Astral Talisman.
Flawless tourmaline handcrafted
in 18k gold 'herb' ring.
Piece no.341

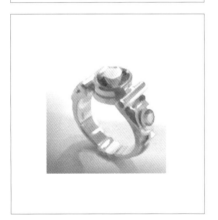

With the aid of computers we personally design every single piece of jewelry produced by AGT

We only produce a few pieces of every design. Thus all our products are totally unique

Each piece sold receives a stamp with its individual number

We started with number one three years ago and have now surpassed number 1,500

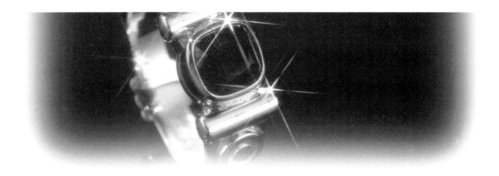

Jupiter Astral Talisman.
Flawless citrine handcrafted
in 21k gold. Piece no.150

The final product is issued a
comprehensive document
stating the astrological and
other particulars pertaining to
the gems in the setting and the
design of the piece, as well as
AGT's guarantee for the quality
of the stone, cut, gold content
and craftsmanship.
It also states its individual
mantra, to be recited on the
appropriate day and time, before
using a new talisman

ASTRAL
GEMSTONE
TALISMANS
The Ultimate in Personalized Planetary Jewelry

Piece # 1160
Mercury Astral Talisman

te of Au

In order to provide the reader with some clear cut insights regarding the practical personal use of astrologically potent gems, the following chapter gives concrete examples of how various types of stones may be employed to offset and counterbalance unfavorable astrological influences in a person's life. All of these anecdotes are drawn from actual cases known to the author or recorded in authenticated texts.

Rahu Astral Talisman.
Flawless hessonite & herb
capsule set in 21k gold.
Piece no.657

X
Gemstone Narratives

THE stories recounted below are true-life examples of how the astral powers of gemstones may be utilized to counteract the undesirable influences of afflicted planets in individual horoscopes by strengthening one's strong planets or, in some cases, one's weak planets. If you suffer from chronic physical or psychic ailments which no physician or medicine has been able to remedy, perhaps the problem lies in a critical deficiency, excess, or imbalance of astral energies in your aura. Any qualified sidereal astrologer can determine what gems will best suit one's needs.

Ruby: The following is a gemstone story from my own experience. The lesson I learned is that only 'good' quality gems are 'lucky'. In 1975 I was residing in the ancient Himalayan Village of *Dhulikhel*, Nepal when I received an urgent telegram from my old friend Sam. His message was simple: **"Discovered Ruby Mine, Come Immediately"** and it ended with a contact in *Hyderabad*, South India.

When I arrived, Sam showed me 'buckets' with rough and cut rubies soaking in jasmine oil. He also showed me an old Sanskrit text which described the mythical origins of the principal gemstones and certain guide lines on their use. One of the verses stated that flawless gems had auspicious talismanic powers, but defective stones were evil and inauspicious. As they didn't have high-powered microscopes in the ancient times it stood to reason that flawless meant 'eye-clean'. In any case, these secret, Hyderabad rubies were definitely **not** eye-clean.

The story unfolded of a 'cursed' Indian family who had discover a huge deposit of 'red corundum' on their property. Fearing the Government, they keep their secret until they ran into good-old Sam who offered to help. He promptly enlisted the financial assistance of (Ex-Beatle) George Harrison and actor Peter Sellers. With this money, he was setting up private cutting and polishing factories and he needed me to visit Bangkok and check out the possibilities. So with five kilos of rough rubies I proceeded to Thailand where I had the stones cut. In the meantime, Sam had exported an enormous amount of rough and cut gems out of India and taken them to New York, the Mecca of Money.

In America he promptly joined forces with unsavory characters of every description and bought two pet lions. Shortly thereafter he returned with his new friends to "really open up the deposit" where they hoped to find some 'clear' rubies. To make a long story short, the whole thing was a fiasco, trunk loads of rough rubies were confiscated, and Sam left India, bitterly diappointed with the whole scheme. Oh! I forgot to mention, one of the pet lions fell from a seventh story Manhattan window and went splat, leaving
Sam with a broken marriage
and shattered dreams.

In the meantime, I took the cut rubies to Bali where I promptly sold everything to the local tourists. I then returned to India, paid the *Hyderabad* family for their rubies and proceeded to Nepal to meet the King. The occasion was the grand-opening of a primary school which I had financed in *Dhulikhel*. At this point my business went sour, I was cheated by a Nepali partner, I was cheated again by my American partner, and when *Kali Baba's* curse descended on the Nepali man I knew it was time to move on. The first thing I did was to bury every last one of those flawed rubies still in my possession. And that is my advice to anyone who shows me a really 'flawed' gemstone: **bury it!** I remembered the old verse from the ancient *Garuda-puranam* which stated that flawed stones are bad luck while eye-clean gems are so auspicious that great sages and royalty of all ages eagerly sought them out.

Moral: Only 'eye-clean' gems are helpful and attractive, while visibly flawed gems are defective and disturbing. Amen!

Ruby Story Two: Some years ago, a prominent Bombay businessman suddenly contracted a chronic fever with dangerously high temperatures which persisted day and night. The best physicians in the city were summoned to his bedside to diagnose and treat his condition, but all to no avail. They tried modern Western and traditional Indian cures, but his condition grew steadily worse until he became partially paralyzed and permanently bedridden. After all medical options had failed, a prominent sidereal astrologer was invited to examine him. Charting the patient's horoscope, the astrologer determined that man had just entered a major Sun period in his life, and glimmering on the man's right hand the astrologer noticed a very fine, large red ruby set in a ring. The astrologer then informed the patient that in addition to having an exalted Sun in his chart, he was just entering a major Sun period and thus the ruby on his hand was attracting a critical surplus of Sun energy. The hot, radiant energy of the Sun, transmitted into the man's system by the flawless ruby on his hand, was causing his persistent fever. The patient removed the ring and completely recovered his health, without resorting to any medication whatsoever.

Sun Astral Talisman. Flawless ruby handcrafted in 18k gold. Piece no.333

Pearl: In Kanpur, India, there lived a university scholar who suffered from painful blisters all over his face. He tried various remedies and potions, but nothing alleviated his affliction. Subsequently, a careful examination of his horoscope revealed that his energy system was being severely afflicted by the unfavorable position of Mars in his horoscope. In addition to being ruled by fire, Mars also governs the face and is generally associated with boils. He was advised to strengthen the Moon's influence by wearing a fine pearl set in silver, and though he felt skeptical about such traditional astro-therapy, since all else had failed to effect a cure, he decided to try the gem therapy as a last resort. Within one month of wearing the pearl set in silver, the man's ailment gradually subsided, the boils on his face disappeared, and he fully recovered his health.

The Moon god Chandra, of Sanskrit creation, here representing the jewels of the Moon

Moonstone: *Testimonial by Ms. Chou Tung of Taiwan:* In June, 1992, when we were living in Thailand, my husband purchased an astral gemstone talisman for me, to protect me from accidents and unseen negative forces. It was a beautiful moonstone, set in a ring of white gold. Two months later, in August, I went back to Taiwan by myself in order to visit my family. My three sisters all remarked on the beauty of my new ring. Then one evening about a week later, one of my sisters noticed a big crack running down the middle of my moonstone and brought it to my attention. Sure enough there was a new crack in it, but no one could figure out why, and so we all went to sleep and forgot about it.

Next morning, they wanted to look at the cracked moonstone in the sunlight, but when I reached to take the ring off my finger, it was gone! Somehow it had disappeared from my finger overnight. We searched the bed, the floor, and the entire house, but there was no sign of it.

That same morning a friend of mine came to pick me up in his car to go shopping with a bunch of old friends. About 15 minutes later, I suddenly remembered that I had to stop at the airlines office to arrange my return flight to Thailand, so I asked my friend to drop me off there. He offered to wait, but I didn't want to inconvenience him and my other friends, so I told them to go on without me, and that I would meet them later for lunch. So they drove off without me, and a few minutes later they were involved in a serious automobile accident in which everyone in the car was badly injured and hospitalized. My friend who was driving was still in the hospital six months later and almost lost his leg.

When I heard the news about the accident later that day, I immediately thought about the crack in my ring and its subsequent disappearance the night before the accident, because I'd heard similar stories about astral talismans 'deflecting' bad luck and averting unforeseen disasters. When I returned to Thailand a few weeks later and told my husband what had happened, the first thing he did was pick up the phone and order another astral talisman ring for me!

Moon Astral Talisman.
Flawless moonstone
handcrafted in 21k
yellow gold. Piece
no.853

Yellow Sapphire: There was a married woman living in India who left her husband because she felt convinced that he no longer loved her. After moving back to her parents' home, she contacted a well-known astrologer to discuss her matrimonial problem. After casting her horoscope and reviewing her chart, the astrologer informed her that the situation was due entirely to the weak position of Jupiter in her horoscope. In order to strengthen her Jupiter and attract this jovial planet's beneficent energy into her system, he advised her to obtain and wear a flawless yellow sapphire of over three carats in weight. Her parents promptly purchased this gem for her and had it mounted in a gold ring. Wearing this ring, she then returned to her husband's home, and through the power of Jupiter's energy attracted by her new ring she soon regained her husband's love and affection and subsequently bore him two fine children.

Jupiter Astral Talisman.
Flawless yellow beryl
handcrafted in 18k
white & yellow gold.
Piece no.489

Rahu Astral Talisman.
Flawless hessonite & herb
chambers handcrafted in
18k white gold.
Piece no.608

Hessonite: *The following story is also drawn from my own personal experience.*

In 1976, while staying on the Indonesia island of Bali, where I was having an extensive collection of unique astral jewelry crafted by goldsmiths there, I was introduced to a young American living on this island. His nickname was 'Abdula' due to his dark complexion, and he was known as an inveterate, chronic gambler. I informed Abdula that the gem hessonite, when flawless, was renowned in traditional Hindu lore as a lucky charm for gamblers, owing to its relationship with the fickle planet Rahu. I happened to have an exceptionally fine specimen of hessonite with me, which I'd recently obtained in Sri Lanka. Intrigued with the idea of owning a gem he bought the stone and asked me to have it properly set in a ring for him. So I designed a special astral ring in pure silver, complete with the appropriate herbal ashes sealed into tiny tubes next to the stone, and sold this talisman to him for $400. When I went to deliver the ring, Abdula was deeply engaged in a serious, high-stakes game of backgammon with several other people. He told his fellow gamblers about the lucky ring, and they all scoffed at the idea of such a powerful talisman. So right then and there he slipped the ring onto his finger and decided to test its purported power. To everyone's incredulous amazement (and to my own great relief), Abdula won the price of the ring in the very first game, and immediately I received three new orders from the other players!

*Mercury Astral
Talismans. Flawless,
matching peridots
& diamonds
handcrafted in 21k
gold. Piece nos.195,
196 & 197*

Emerald: Another example from India, where the astral powers of gemstones are taken for granted, recounts how faith in astral gemology can save a person from premature death. In Uttar Pradesh, India, there lived a gentlemen who habitually wore an emerald of good quality, based on the advice of his personal astrologer. One day, while purchasing an airline ticket to Bombay, he happened to notice that the emerald in his ring had developed a small crack. Taking this sign as a bad omen, he immediately canceled his flight reservation, and the airplane took off without him. The plane crashed, and everyone on board perished!

Diamond: *Another incident from the authors own personal experience took place in 1975, in Kathmandu, Nepal.* I was visiting the jewelry shop of a Nepali friend on New Road, when an Indian diamond smuggler came into the shop to sell some of his gems to my friend. On the man's finger I noticed a ring set with an unusually large diamond. I asked to see the ring, and examining the diamond in magnification through a jewelers loop, I noticed that it was tainted with a red spot. I mentioned this to the man, and told him and my friend what I had heard about such stones while previously traveling in Jaipur. According to ancient Hindu gem lore, wearing a diamond with a red spot inside it would bring premature death to whoever wore it, even to a highly accomplished yogi who had already 'conquered death'. My Nepali friend nodded gravely and said that he too had heard this tale, but the Indian smuggler, who should have known better, simply laughed and dismissed it all as mere myth. Later on that day I returned to my friend's jewelry shop to pick up a piece of jewelry I'd ordered, but to my surprise the shop was closed, and it remained, closed for two more days. When it finally reopened, my friend informed me that the Indian fellow with the flawed diamond ring had been killed in an accident right in front of the shop shortly after our conversation there!

Venus Astral Talisman.
Piece 908. Flawless
zircon & diamond
handcrafted in
21k gold

Cat's Eye : There was an American who, due to his black-market dealings, had reason to fear the government. To off-set this danger he purchased a flawless precious cat's eye gem of four carats in weight. About six months later this person was caught red-handed by the authorities. Inspite of this he was able to cooperate with the government and eventually ended up with nothing more than probation. Thereafter he was allowed to move far away from his home where he remains free from reprisals. The cat's eye energy of the Planet *Ketu* had helped him overcome his negative *karma* of government punishment as well as any danger from hidden enemies he had to fear as a result of his cooperation. A subsequent study of his sidereal horoscope revealed the position of *Ketu* (the diety ruling cat's eye gems) to be very negative. The boost in his *Ketu* energy almost immediately proved harmful. It was the superb quality of the gem which must have saved the day.

Ketu Astral Talisman.
Flawless cat's eye & herb tubes
handcrafted in 21k gold.
Piece no.858

Ketu Astral Talisman.
Piece no.218. Flawless
cat's eye & diamonds
handcrafted in 21k gold.

Cat's Eye Story Two: An old Romanian tale relates the story of a princess named *Vrina* who fell into abject poverty due to a severe famine in her land. The only possession which she managed to retain was a golden lizard pendant set with eyes of cat's eye chrysoberyl. This pendent had always been her lucky charm, and a famous mystic had told her never under any circumstances to sell it, for it possessed a special power which would enable her to communicate with animals in times of crisis, and thereby save her from ruin. When all of her possessions save for the lizard pendant were gone, she broke down and wept in despair. At that very moment, a lizard with green eyes similar to the color of cat's eye approached and "spoke" to her. The lizard communicated the information that she would find her salvation in the dry bed of the river. So she went to the river with her subjects and upon excavating the dry bed they discovered a rich deposit of fine cat's eye gems, which quickly restored the prosperity of her kingdom.

115

Blue Sapphire: The ancient Sanskrit scriptures known as the *Puranas* contain a well-known story regarding the astral powers of blue sapphires. One day, the great King *Dushyanta* was hunting in the forest when he met and instantly fell in love with a young girl named *Shakuntala*, who was the daughter of a powerful sage living as an ascetic yogi in the wilderness. Wishing to marry her, the King gave her a beautiful blue sapphire ring to mark their engagement, and he told her to come to his palace whenever she felt ready to marry. One morning a few month later, as she stood by the river bank drawing water for her father, the sapphire ring slipped off her finger, fell into the river, and was promptly swallowed by a fish. When later she went to visit the King at his palace to consent to his proposal, the King did not recognize her, nor could he recall his promise of marriage. Deeply distressed, she returned sadly to her father's hut in the forest.

A few months later, the fish which swallowed the ring was caught by a local fisherman, who found the precious sapphire inside its stomach. Thinking that this might be important, the fisherman took the ring to the King. The moment the King set eyes on the stone he immediately remembered Shakuntala and his proposal of marriage to her. He sent for her, and soon they were married and lived a long happy life together, thanks to the precious gem which consummated their destiny.

◆————————————

Red Coral: Not long ago a Thai lady night-club owner came to visit our Astral Gemstone Talismans Showroom in Bangkok. While waiting for her horoscope to be cast she saw a Mars bangle set with a large red coral. She immediately put on the bangle and left the shop saying she would return to pay for the piece. Not more than 10 minutes later she returned the bangle explaining that she just had a heated argument with her boyfriend who strongly objected to her wearing the red coral. Upon checking her horoscope we found that Mars was posited in the sign of Leo, a very strong, fiery position, signifying (among other things) romantic conflicts. Increasing her Mars energy by wearing the large red coral had an immediately violent effect on her relationship, which was painfully apparent.

◆————————————

The Shyamantaka Gem

The following is my all-time favorite gemstone story. This legend is derived from the 10th Canto of the great *Bhagavata Maha-purana : book 10, chapter VII.* Over 5,000 years ago, at the end of the *Dvarpara-yuga* or the 'Copper Age', the 8th Incarnation of Lord *Vishnu* appeared on the Earth as Lord *Krishna*. During the latter part of His sojourn on this planet *Krishna* was involved in a misunderstanding over a wonderful ruby known as the *Shyamantaka* gem.

There was a King named *Satrajit* who was a devotee of *Surya*, the Sun-god. After many years of worship King *Satrajit* was finally blessed by the Sun-god who gave him a fabulous ruby as a reward for his dedication. This ruby was named *'Shyamantaka'* and it had the power to produce one hundred seventy pounds of gold daily for it's owner. Such was the great brilliance of this gem that people mistook King *Satrajit* to be the Sun-god himself where ever he wore the jewel. One day *Satrajit* went to visit Lord *Krishna* on His island Kingdom of *Dvaraka*. *Krishna*, understanding *Satrajit's* inflated ego and attachment, asked him for the gem. When *Satrajit* refused, *Krishna* relented and said nothing further about the matter. But the devoted denizens of *Dvaraka* were surprised and soon gossip spread throughout the Kingdom.

Later, the brother of *Satrajit*, *Prasena*, borrowed the gem and went boldly into the forest to hunt. Unknown to anyone, *Prasena* was killed by a great lion who was in turn killed by *Jambavan*, the King of Bears, who took the *Shyamantaka* jewel into his cave and gave it to his child to play with. Soon the news of the gems disappearance turned into ugly rumors that perhaps *Krishna* was responsible for the theft. Sensing the people's doubt, Lord *Krishna* ventured out to search for the gem accompanied by a large group of followers. Later they found the dead bodies of both *Prasena* and the lion. Finally they came to the cave of *Jambavan* and *Krishna* entered the cave alone, leaving his associates out side. Seeing *Krishna* and not knowing his true greatness, *Jambavan* engaged Him in mortal combat. After the fighting had continued unabated for over 14 days and nights *Jambavan* began losing strength while *Krishna* was still strong and getting stronger. At this point *Jambavan* realized *Krishna's* true identity and offered *Krishna* the jewel and his daughter in apology.

116

Lord Krishna, here in the
form of the flutist-charmer
is, through vedic literature,
intimately linked to the
power of flawless gems

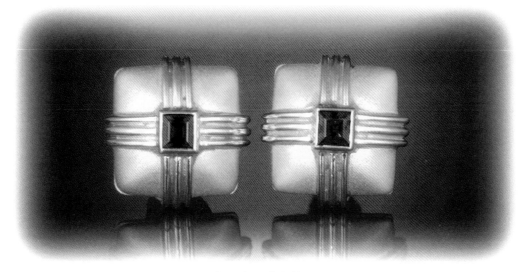

Sun Astral Talisman.
Flawless red spinels
handcrafted into
18k gold earrings.
Pieces no.745

When *Krishna* returned triumphantly to *Dvaraka* the truth became known and the Lord returned the *Shyamantaka* gem to King *Satrajit*. The legend of the gem continues with *Satrajit* getting killed, etc, etc., but the most memorable part of the saga involves Lord *Sri Krishna*.

One of the most esoteric aspects of 'Planetary Gemology' deals with the Planetary Deity ruling each gem. These *Graha-devas* belong to the Cosmic Hierarchy and their influence is felt according to the angle or *rasi* (sign) and *bhava* (house) they occupy in one's horoscope as well as their **major planetary periods** (about 70% influence) and their **minor planetary periods** (about 30% influence). There are many other considerations including **Sun periods** (30 days), **moon periods**, **aspects**, **lord ownership**, **transits**, and many other more subtle points which involve understanding the horoscope as a whole. In the East the concept and belief in the *devas* or 'cosmic hierarchy' is deeply rooted in ancient *Vedic* tradition. The use of gems as a way of invoking each stone's **ruling planetary deity** is still prevalent. This consideration is the most esoteric aspect of 'gem therapy' and is not for those who do not believe in *karma* or rebirth.

These are only a small handful of the many amazing cases associated with the potent therapeutic powers of precious gemstones, which can influence a person's health and longevity for better or for worse by attracting and amplifying various types of cosmic energies from the stars and planets. In some cases, It's the critical deficiency of a particular type of astral energy which causes the problem, while in other cases it's an over-abundance and imbalance of energies due to the presence of inappropriate or flawed gemstones on a person's body.

If you've been suffering from chronic physical or psychic afflictions for which conventional medical remedies are consistently ineffective, or if you experience persistent runs of bad luck, you may wish to consider trying to correct the situation through astral-therapy by consulting a qualified sidereal astrologer, then obtaining and wearing the astrological gemstones or talismans which he or she prescribes. The answers to many of our most common problem are literally 'written in the stars', and astrological gemstones, which function somewhat like radio crystal receivers to attract, modulate, and amplify the invisible energies which rain down on us from the cosmos, can bring those energies and those answers down to earth.

In conclusion I would like to point out that gemstones for planets which are harmful in one's horoscope and also gemstones of planets which are cruel by nature, like Saturn, Mars, *Rahu* & *Ketu*, may be donated to advantage by someone wishing to placate these planets through the recitation of mantras and performance of certain acts of sacrifice. Used as a medium for *graha-puja* or planetary solicitation these otherwise harmful gems help to magnify one's prayer. Anyone who is not willing to perform the requisite sacred rites may well come to grief by using gems which represent a harmful planetary influence in one's life. Therefore, the idea of pacifying planets thru the use of gems, can be done, provided one obtain the necessary information in order to carry out the rituals correctly. Otherwise, one should normally avoid gems which represent a harmful influence on one's life.

◆━━━━━━━━

*We are proud to be associated with experienced astrologers (Jyotishacaryas) such as **Pandit Vidyadhar Shukla** (pictured above), who is a renowned Vedic scholar as also the Chief Brahmin Priest of Thailand*

XI
The Final Word on 'Crystals'

IN recent years, occult talismans of quartz crystal have become increasingly popular throughout the Western world. Believing that such crystals provide a panacea for all ills, an infinite source of cosmic energy, and absolute protection against evil spirits, people wear them in rings, necklaces, bracelets, pendants, and key-chains, without taking into consideration their intrinsic gemological quality or their astrological side-effects. Furthermore, they mistakenly believe that only quartz crystals (also known as 'rock crystals') provide the desired power and protection.

The fact is that clear quartz crystals are only the most common variety among many different types of gem crystals. All precious gemstones, except for those composed of organic matter such as coral and pearl, belong to one of six major categories of natural crystal, and almost all gem crystals are far more rare than the common clear quartz variety. Many precious gems are actually natural quartz crystals structurally fused with various trace elements that add color to the stone. For example, amethyst is actually purple quartz, and citrine is simply yellow quartz.

As discussed in previous chapters, all of the ancient gemological teachings of the East place prime importance on the color and the quality of gem crystals. The color determines which of the nine planets rules the gem, and the quality determines whether a gemstone transmits the positive or negative energies of it's associated planet. Clear colorless gems such as diamond and quartz crystal, for example, transmit the energy and astral influence of the planet Venus, while red gem crystals such as ruby and garnet attract the energy and influence of the Sun. However, it is the tone of the color and the gemological quality of the crystal which determine how well a particular gem functions as an astral talisman. Even colorless quartz must be 'crystal clear' and free of flaws in order to conduct the auspicious energy of Venus to the person who wears it.

An expensive astral ruby (left) or the astral spinel (right); either makes as effective a Talisman as would, for instance, a flawless red garnet

The ancient *Vedic* texts of India ascribe the mythological origins of clear quartz crystals to the semen of *Vala*, and therefore this sort of colorless gemstone governs sexuality and the entire realm of sensual activity. It is interesting to note that the planet Venus, which is associated with colorless crystals, has always been regarded as the planet of love and sex in both Eastern and Western astrology.

The current fad for talismans of quartz rock crystal has given rise to the popular misconception that only colorless quartz has the capacity to transmit auspicious cosmic energy. Not only is this a fallacy, it can also bring great misfortune to people by attracting the wrong type of energy into their systems. One should only wear gems which transmit the planetary energies appropriate to one's individual horoscope. Diamonds, for example, have always been regarded as 'a girl's best friend' in the Western world, but according to *Vedic* reference, diamonds bring nothing but misery to most women. The Western view is based entirely on commercial considerations, while the Eastern view is rooted in ancient esoteric teachings that have withstood the test of time, as illustrated in the true stories presented in the previous chapter.

After selecting the appropriate type of gem according to its color and planetary association, the most important factor to consider when purchasing a gem is its crystal **clarity**. The importance of flawless clarity in gems cannot be overemphasized, for only the finest quality crystals transmit the positive energies of their associated planets. Flawed stones work in reverse, i.e., they transmit flawed energy and therefore bring misfortune rather than auspicious influences. Note the fate of the Indian smuggler who sported the flawed diamond in flagrant disregard for the advice of the ancient sages.

If you cannot afford the price of a flawless ruby or diamond, you may opt instead for a flawless but far less expensive red garnet or colorlessquartz crystal. All of the astrological planets have several varieties of gemstone which transmit their cosmic energies. These are all listed in this book under each planet, beginning with the primary, most precious gems and followed by secondary, less expensive types. It's better, for example, to wear a flawless red garnet than a flawed ruby. People interested in enhancing their lives through the auspicious cosmic energies transmitted by planetary gemstones should select only flawless specimens. It is in fact better to wear no gems at all than to wear flawed stones. But since every planet offers a variety of gems from 'first class' to 'economy class', one may easily pick a flawless gem which suits one's individual budget as well as one's horoscope.

Aum Tat Sat!

Venus Astral Talisman. Flawless diamonds handcrafted in 18k gold. Piece no.138

(right) A sample of possibly flawless quartz crystal.

121

Planetary Mantras, Charity & Fasting

Practices for the attraction of auspicious planets and mitigation of
harmful planetary influences, which may be combined with the use of fine,
natural gemstones for enhanced effect.

Propitiation of the Sun (Sunday)

Charity: Donate a ruby or another fine red jewel like red spinel, gold, copper, wheat, or sugar candy to a middle aged male government leader at 12:00 noon on a Sunday.

Fasting: On Sundays, especially during Sun transits and major or minor Sun periods.

Mantra: To be chanted on Sunday morning at sunrise, especially during Sun transits and major or minor Sun periods:

Atha Surya-astottara-shata-nama-vali
(The 108 names of *Surya*)

Aum arunaya namah
Aum sharanyaya namah
Aum karuna-rasa-sindhave namah
Aum asmanabalaya namah
Aum arta-raksa-kaya namah
Aum adityaya namah
Aum adi-bhutaya namah
Aum akhila-gamavedine namah
Aum acyutaya namah
Aum akhilagnaya namah
Aum anantaya namah
Aum inaya namah
Aum visva-rupaya namah
Aum ijyaya namah
Aum indraya namah
Aum bhanave namah
Aum indriramandiraptaya namah
Aum vandaniyaya namah
Aum ishaya namah
Aum suprasannaya namah
Aum sushilaya namah
Aum suvarcase namah
Aum vasupradaya namah
Aum vasave namah
Aum vasudevaya namah
Aum ujjvalaya namah
Aum ugra-rupaya namah
Aum urdhvagaya namah
Aum vivasvate namah
Aum udhatkiranajalaya namah
Aum hrishikesaya namah
Aum urjasvalaya namah
Aum viraya namah
Aum nirjaraya namah
Aum jayaya namah

Sun Astral Talisman.
Flawless ruby
handcrafted in 21k
gold. Piece no.830

122

Aum urudvayavirnimuktanijasarakrashivandyaya namah
Aum rugdhantre namah
Aum kraksacakracaraya namah
Aum krajusvabhavavittaya namah
Aum nityastutyaya namah
Aum krukaramatrikavarnarupaya ujjvalatejase namah
Aum kruksadhinathamitraya namah
Aum pushakaraksaya namah
Aum luptadantaya namah
Aum shantaya namah
Aum kantidaya namah
Aum dhanaya namah
Aum kanatkanaka sushanaya namah
Aum khalotaya namah
Aum lunit-akhila-daityaya namah
Aum satya-ananda-svarupine namah
Aum apavarga-pradaya namah
Aum arta-sharanyaya namah
Aum ekakine namah
Aum bhagavate namah
Aum sushtisthityantakarine namah
Aum gunatmane namah
Aum dhrinibhrite namah
Aum brihate namah
Aum brahmane namah
Aum esvaryadaya namah
Aum sharvaya namah
Aum haridashvaya namah
Aum shauraye namah
Aum dashadiksam-prakashaya namah
Aum bhakta-vashyaya namah
Aum ojaskaraya namah
Aum jayine namah
Aum jagad-ananda-hetave namah
Aum taya janma-mrtyu-jara-vyadhi-varji
aounnatyapadasamcararathasthaya-asuraraye namah
Aum kamaniyakagaya namah
Aum abjaballabhaya namah
Aum antar-bahih prakashaya namah
Aum acintyaya namah
Aum atma-rupine namah
Aum acyutaya namah
Aum amareshaya namah
Aum parasmai jyotishe namah
Aum ahaskaraya namah
Aum ravaye namah
Aum haraye namah
Aum param-atmane namah
Aum tarunaya namah
Aum tarenyaya namah
Aum grahanam pataye namah
Aum bhaskaraya namah
Aum adimadhyantara-hitaya namah
Aum saukhyapradaya namah
Aum sakalajagatam pataye namah
Aum suryaya namah
Aum kavaye namah
Aum narayanaya namah
Aum pareshaya namah
Aum tejorupaya namah

Sun Astral Talisman.
Flawless Burmese red
spinel handcrafted in
21k gold. Piece no.70

Aum shrim hiranyagarbhaya namah
Aum hrim sampatkaraya namah
Aum aim istarthadaya namah
Aum am suprasannaya namah
Aum shrimate namah
Aum shreyase namah
Aum saukhyadayine namah
Aum diptamurtaye namah
Aum nikhilagamavedhyaya namah
Aum nityanandaya namah

Surya seed mantra: *Aum hram hrim hraum sah suryaya namah.*

Result: The planetary deity *Surya* is pleased increasing courage and notoriety.

Propitiation of the Moon (Monday)

Charity: Donate a pearl or moonstone, conch shell, silver, water, cow's milk or white rice to a female leader on Monday evening during the waxing moon.

Fasting: On Mondays, especially during Moon transits and major or minor Moon periods.

Mantra: To be chanted on Monday evening, especially during major or minor Moon periods:

Atha chandra-astottara-shata-nama-vali
(The 108 names of *Chandra*)

Aum srimate namah
Aum shasha-dharaya namah
Aum chandraya namah
Aum tara-adhishaya namah
Aum nisha-karaya namah
Aum sugha-nighaye namah
Aum sadaradhya namah
Aum sat-pataye namah
Aum sadhu-pujitaya namah
Aum jitendriyaya namah
Aum jayodhyogaya namah
Aum jyotish-cakra-pravartakaya namah
Aum vikartananujaya namah
Aum viraya namah
Aum vishveshaya namah
Aum vidusham pataye namah
Aum doshakaraya namah
Aum dushta-duraya namah
Aum pushtimate namah
Aum shishta-palakaya namah
Aum ashta-murti-priyaya namah
Aum anantaya namah
Aum kashta-daru-kutharakaya namah
Aum sva-prakashaya namah
Aum prakash-atmane namah
Aum dyu-caraya namah
Aum deva-bhojanaya namah

Moon Astral Talisman.
Flawless moonstone
handcrafted in 21k
gold. Piece no.144

124

Aum kala-dharaya namah
Aum kala-hetave namah
Aum kama-krite namah
Aum kama-dayakaya namah
Aum mrityu-saharakaya namah
Aum amartyaya namah
Aum nityanushthana-dayakaya namah
Aum ksapa-karaya namah
Aum ksina-papaya namah
Aum ksaya-vriddhi-samanvitaya namah
Aum jaivatrikaya namah
Aum shucaye namah
Aum shubhraya namah
Aum jayine namah
Aum jaya-phala-pradaya namah
Aum sudha-mayaya namah
Aum sura-svamine namah
Aum bhaktanam-ishtha-dayakaya namah
Aum bukti-daya namah
Aum mukti-daya namah
Aum bhadraya namah
Aum bhakta-daridhya bhanjanaya namah
Aum sama-gana-priyaya namah
Aum sarva-raksakaya namah
Aum sagarodbhavaya namah
Aum bhayanta-krite namah
Aum bhakti-gamyaya namah
Aum bhava-bandha-vimocakaya namah
Aum jagat-prakasa-kiranaya namah
Aum jagad-ananda-kiranaya namah
Aum nissapatnaya namah
Aum niraharaya namah
Aum nirvikaraya namah
Aum niramayaya namah
Aum bhu-cchaya-cchaditaya namah
Aum bhavyaya namah
Aum bhuvana-prati-palakaya namah
Aum sakalarti-haraya namah
Aum saumya-janakaya namah
Aum sadhu-vanditaya namah
Aum sarvagama-jnaya namah
Aum sarva-jnaya namah
Aum sanakadi-muni-stutaya namah
Aum sita-chatra-dhvajopetaya namah
Aum sitangaya namah
Aum sita-bhusanaya namah
Aum sveta-malyambara-dharaya namah
Aum sveta-gandhanulepanaya namah
Aum dasasva-ratha-samrudhaya namah
Aum danda-pananye namah
Aum dhanur-dharaya namah
Aum kunda-pusyojjvalakaraya namah
Aum nayanabja-samudbhavaya namah
Aum atreya-gotra-jaya namah
Aum atyanta-vinayaya namah
Aum priya-dayakaya namah
Aum karuna-rasa-sampurnaya namah
Aum karkata-prabhave namah
Aum avyayaya namah
Aum catur-ashrasanarudhaya namah
Aum caturaya namah

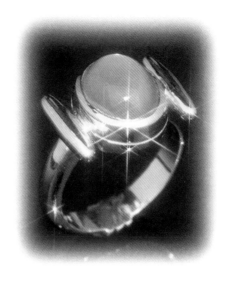

Moon Astral Talisman.
Flawless moonstone
handcrafted in 18k gold.
Piece no.610

125

Aum divya-vahanaya namah
Aum vivasvan mandalajneya-vasaya namah
Aum vasu-samrddhi-daya namah
Aum mahesvara-priyaya namah
Aum dantaya namah
Aum meru-gotra-pradaksinaya namah
Aum graha-mandala-madhyasthaya namah
Aum grasitarkaya namah
Aum grahadhipaya namah
Aum dvija-rajaya namah
Aum dyuti-lakaya namah
Aum dvibhujaya namah
Aum dvija-pujitaya namah
Aum audumbara-nagavasaya namah
Aum udaraya namah
Aum rohini-pataye namah
Aum nityodayaya namah
Aum muni-stutyaya namah
Aum nityananda-phala-pradaya namah
Aum sakalahladana-karaya namah
Aum palashedhma-priyaya namah

Chandra seed mantra: *Aum sram srim sraum sah chandraya namah.*

Result: The planetary deity *Chandra* is pleased increasing mental health and peace of mind.

Moon Astral Talisman.
Flawless moonstone
talisman handcrafted in
21k gold. Piece no.447

Propitiation of Mars (Tuesday)

Charity: Donate a red coral, wheat bread, sweets made from sugar mixed with white sesamum seeds, or masoor dal (red lentils) to a celibate on Tuesday at noon.

Fasting: On Tuesdays, especially during Mars transits and major or minor Mars periods.

Mantra: To be chanted on Tuesday, one hour after sunrise, especially during major or minor Mars periods:

Angaraka-astottara-shata-nama-vali
(The 108 names of *Mangala*)

Aum mahisutaya namah
Aum maha-bhagaya namah
Aum mangalaya namah
Aum mangala-pradaya namah
Aum maha-virayam namah
Aum maha-shuraya namah
Aum maha-balaparakramaya namah
Aum maharoudraya namah
Aum mahabhadraya namah
Aum mananiyaya namah
Aum dayakaraya namah
Aum manadaya namah
Aum aparvanaya namah
Aum kruraya namah
Aum tapa-traya-vivarjitaya namah
Aum supratipaya namah
Aum sutamrakshaya namah
Aum subrahmanyaya namah
Aum sukhapradaya namah
Aum vakra-stambhadi-gamanaya namah
Aum varenyaya namah
Aum varadaya namah
Aum sukhine namah
Aum virabhadraya namah
Aum virupaksaya namah
Aum vidurasthaya namah
Aum vibhavasave namah
Aum naksatra-cakra-samcarine namah
Aum ksatrapaya namah
Aum ksatravarjitaya namah
Aum ksayavriddhivinirmuktaya namah
Aum ksama-yuktaya namah
Aum vicaksanaya namah
Aum aksinaphaladaya namah
Aum caturvarga-phala-pradaya namah
Aum vitaragaya namah
Aum vitabhayaya namah
Aum vijvaraya namah
Aum vishva-karanaya namah
Aum naksatra-rashisancaraya namah
Aum nanabhayanikrintanaya namah
Aum vandarujanamandaraya namah
Aum vakrakuncitamurddhajaya namah
Aum kamaniyaya namah
Aum dayasaraya namah
Aum kanatkanakabhusanaya namah

Mars Astral Talisman.
Flawless coral handcrafted
in 18k gold. Piece no.662.

127

Aum bhayaghnaya namah
Aum bhavya-phaladaya namah
Aum bhakta-bhaya-varapradaya namah
Aum shatru-hantre' namah
Aum shamope'taya namah
Aum sharanagataposhanaya namah
Aum sahasine' namah
Aum sad-gunadhyaksaya namah
Aum sadhave' namah
Aum samaradurjayaya namah
Aum dushtha-duraya namah
Aum shishtha-pujyaya namah
Aum sarva-kashtha-nivarakaya namah
Aum dushche'shtha-varakaya namah
Aum duhkha-bhanjanaya namah
Aum durdharaya namah
Aum haraye namah
Aum dhu-svapna-hamtre' namah
Aum dur-dharshaya namah
Aum dushta-garva-vimocanaya namah
Aum bharadvaja-kulam-adbhutaya namah
Aum bhu-sutaya namah
Aum bhavya-bhushanaya namah
Aum raktam-varaya namah
Aum rakta-vapushe' namah
Aum bhakta-palana-tatparaya namah
Aum catur-bhujaya namah
Aum gada-dharine' namah
Aum mesha-vahaya namah
Aum sitashanaya namah
Aum shakti-shula-dharaya namah
Aum shaktaya namah
Aum shastra-vidya-visharadaya namah
Aum tarkakaya namah
Aum tamasa-dharaya namah
Aum tapasvine' namah
Aum tamra-locanaya namah
Aum taptakancana-samkashaya namah
Aum rakta-kinjalkamannibhaya namah
Aum gotra adhi-devaya namah
Aum gomadhy-acaraya namah
Aum guna-vibhushanaya namah
Aum asrije' namah
Aum angarakaya namah
Aum avanti-desha-adhishaya namah
Aum janardanaya namah
Aum suryayamya-pradeshasthaya namah
Aum ghune' namah
Aum yamya-harin-mukhaya namah
Aum trikona-mandala-gataya namah
Aum tridasha-adhipasannutaya namah
Aum shucaye' namah
Aum shucikaraya namah
Aum shuraya namah
Aum shuci-vashyaya namah
Aum shubha-vahaya namah
Aum mesha-vriscika-rashishaya namah
Aum medhavine' namah

Aum mita-bhashanaya namah
Aum sukha-pradaya namah
Aum surupa-aksaya namah
Aum sarva-bhishta-phala-pradaya namah

Mangala seed mantra: *Aum kram krim kraum sah bhaumaya namah.*

Result: The planetary deity *Mangala* is pleased increasing determination and drive, and protecting one from violence.

Propitiation of Mercury (Wednesday)

Charity: Donate emerald or another fine green gem, small green lentils, a green pumpkin, a goat, or green clothes to a poor student on Wednesday at noon.

Fasting: On Wednesday, especially during Mercury transits and major or minor Mercury periods.

Mantra: To be chanted on Wednesday, two hours after sunrise, especially during major or minor Mercury periods:

Budha-astottara-shata-nama-vali
(The 108 names of *Budha*)

Aum bhudhaya namah
Aum budharcitaya namah
Aum saumyaya namah
Aum saumyachittaya namah
Aum shubha-pradaya namah
Aum drida-brataya namah
Aum hadaphalaya namah
Aum shruti-jala-prabodhakaya namah
Aum satya 'vasaya namah
Aum satya-vacase namah
Aum shreyasam pataye namah
Aum abyayaya namah
Aum soma-jaya namah
Aum sukhadaya namah
Aum shrimate namah
Aum soma-vamsha-pradipa-kaya namah
Aum vedavide namah
Aum veda-tattvashaya namah
Aum vedanta-jnana-bhaskaraya namah
Aum vidya-vicaksanaya namah
Aum vidushe namah
Aum vidvat-pritikaraya namah
Aum krajave namah
Aum vishva-anukula-sancaraya namah
Aum vishesha-vinayanvitaya namah
Aum vividhagamasarajnaya namah
Aum viryavate namah

Mercury Astral Talisman.
Flawless peridot
handcrafted in 18k gold.
Piece no.591

Mercury Astral Talisman.
Flawless peridot handcrafted in
21k gold. Piece no.765

Aum vigatajvaraya namah
Aum trivarga-phaladaya namah
Aum anantaya namah
Aum tridasha-dhipa-pujitaya namah
Aum buddhimate namah
Aum bahu-shastra-jnaya namah
Aum baline namah
Aum bandha-vimocakaya namah
Aum vakativakagamanaya namah
Aum vasavaya namah
Aum vasudhadhipaya namah
Aum prasannavadanaya namah
Aum vandhyaya namah
Aum varenyaya namah
Aum vagvilaksanaya namah
Aum satya-vate namah
Aum satya-samkalpaya namah
Aum satya-bamdhave namah
Aum sadadaraya namah
Aum sarva-roga-prashamanaya namah
Aum sarva-mrityu-nivarakaya namah
Aum vanijyanipunaya namah
Aum vashyaya namah
Aum vatan-gaya namah
Aum vata-roga-hrite' namah
Aum sthulaya namah
Aum sthairya-guna-adhyaksaya namah
Aum sthula-suksma-adi-karanaya namah
Aum aprakashaya namah
Aum prakash-atmane' namah
Aum ghanaya namah
Aum gagana-bhushanaya namah
Aum vidhi-stutyaya namah
Aum visha-laksaya namah
Aum vidvajjana-manoharaya namah
Aum caru-shilaya namah
Aum svaprakashaya namah
Aum capalaya namah
Aum jitendriyaya namah
Aum udan-mukhaya namah
Aum bukhamakkaya namah
Aum magadha-adhi-pataye namah
Aum haraye namah
Aum saumya-vatsara-samjataya namah
Aum soma-priya-karaya namah
Aum mahate namah
Aum sihma-adhirudhaya namah
Aum sarva-jnaya namah
Aum shikhivarnaya namah
Aum shivam-karaya namah
Aum pitambaraya namah
Aum pitavapushe' namah
Aum pitacchatradhvajankitaya
Aum khanga-carma-dharaya namah
Aum karya-kartre' namah
Aum kalushaharakaya namah
Aum atreya-gotra-jaya namah
Aum atyanta-vinayaya namah
Aum vishva-pavanaya namah

Mercury Astral Talisman.
Flawless tourmaline
handcrafted in 21k gold.
Piece no.771

Aum campeya-puspa-samkashaya namah
Aum caranaya namah
Aum caru-bhushanaya namah
Aum vita-ragaya namah
Aum vita-bhayaya namah
Aum vishuddha-kanaka-prabhaya
Aum bandhu-priyaya namah
Aum bandhu-yuktaya namah
Aum bana-mandala—samshritaya namah
Aum arkesana-nivasasthaya tarka-shastra-visharadmaya namah
Aum prashantaya namah
Aum priti-samyuktaya namah
Aum priya-krite' namah
Aum priya-bhushanaya namah
Aum medhavine' namah
Aum madhava-saktaya namah
Aum mithuna-adhi-pataye' namah
Aum sudhiye namah
Aum kanya-rashi-priyaya namah
Aum kama-pradaya namah
Aum ghana-phala-ashrayaya namah

Budha seed mantra*: Aum bram brim braum sah budhaya namah.*

Result: The planetary deity *Budha* is pleased
increasing health and intelligence.

Propitiation of Jupiter (Thursday)

Charity: Donate yellow sapphire or another yellow gem like yellow topaz, a peepal sapling, saffron, turmeric, sugar, a horse, or yellow flowers to a *brahmin* (priest) on Thursday morning.

Fasting: On Thursday, especially during Jupiter transits and major or minor Jupiter periods.

Mantra: To be chanted on Thursday, one hour before sunset, especially during major or minor Jupiter periods:

Gurva-astottara-shata-nama-vali
(The 108 names of *Guru*)

Aum gurave namah
Aum gunakaraya namah
Aum goptre namah
Aum gocaraya namah
Aum gopatipriyaya namah
Aum gunive namah
Aum gunavatam shrepthaya namah
Aum gurunam gurave namah
Aum avyayaya namah

131

Jupiter Astral Talisman.
Flawless yellow beryl &
herb capsules
handcrafted in
18k gold.
Piece no.583

Aum jetre namah
Aum jayantaya namah
Aum jayadaya namah
Aum jivaya namah
Aum anantaya namah
Aum jayavahaya namah
Aum amgirasaya namah
Aum adhvaramaktaya namah
Aum viviktaya namah
Aum adhvarakritparaya namah
Aum vacaspataye namah
Aum vashine namah
Aum vashyaya namah
Aum varishthaya namah
Aum vagvacaksanaya namah
Aum citta-shuddhi-karaya namah
Aum shrimate namah
Aum caitraya namah
Aum citrashikhandijaya namah
Aum brihad-rathaya namah
Aum brihad-bhanave namah
Aum brihas-pataye namah
Aum abhishtadaya namah
Aum suracaryaya namah
Aum suraradhyaya namah
Aum surakaryakritodyamaya namah
Aum girvanaposhakaya namah
Aum dhanyaya namah
Aum gishpataye namah
Aum girishaya namah
Aum anaghaya namah
Aum dhivaraya namah
Aum dhishanaya namah
Aum divya-bhushanaya namah
Aum deva-pujitaya namah
Aum dhanurddharaya namah
Aum daitya-hantre namah
Aum dayasaraya namah
Aum dayakaraya namah
Aum dariddya-nashanaya namah
Aum dhanyaya namah
Aum daksinayanasambhavaya namah
Aum dhanurminadhipaya namah
Aum devaya namah
Aum dhanurbana-dharaya namah
Aum haraye namah
Aum angarovarshasamjataya namah
Aum angirah kulasambhavaya namah
Aum sindhu-desha-adhipaya namah
Aum dhimate namah
Aum svarnakayaya namah
Aum catur-bhujaya namah
Aum heman-gadaya namah
Aum hemavapushe namah
Aum hemabhushanabhushitaya namah
Aum pushyanathaya namah
Aum pushyaragamanimandanamandi kasha-pushpa-samanabhaya namah
Aum indradyamarasamghapaya namah
Aum asamanabalaya namah
Aum satva-guna-sampadvibhavasave bhusurabhishtadaya namah

Aum bhuriyashase namah
Aum punya-vivardhanaya namah
Aum dharma-rupaya namah
Aum dhana-adhyaksaya namah
Aum dhanadaya namah
Aum dharma-palanaya namah
Aum sarva-veda-artha-tattva-jnaya namah
Aum sarva-padvinivarakaya namah
Aum sarva-papa-prashamanaya namah
Aum svramatanugatamaraya namah
rigveda-paragaya namah
Aum riksarashimargapracaravate sada-anandaya namah
Aum satya-samdhaya namah
Aum satya-samkalpa-manasaya namah
Aum sarva-gamajnaya namah
Aum sarva-jnaya namah
Aum sarva-vedanta-vide namah
Aum brahma-putraya namah
Aum brahmaneshaya namah
Aum brahma-vidya-avisharadaya namah
Aum samana-adhi-kanirbhuktaya namah
Aum sarva-loka-vashamvadaya namah
Aum sasura-asura-gandharva-vanditaya satya-bhashanaya namah
Aum brihaspataye namah
Aum suracaryaya namah
Aum dayavate namah
Aum shubha-laksanaya namah
Aum loka-traya-gurave namah
Aum shrimate namah
Aum sarva-gaya namah
Aum sarvato vibhave namah
Aum sarveshaya namah
Aum sarvadatushtaya namah
Aum sarva-daya namah
Aum sarva-pujitaya namah

Guru seed mantra: *Aum gram grim graum sah gurave namah.*

Result: The planetary deity *Brihaspati* is pleased increasing satisfaction and facilitating marriage and childbirth.

Jupiter Astral Talisman. Flawless
yellow sapphires & herb capsule
handcrafted in 21k gold.
Piece no.829

Propitiation of Venus (Friday)

Charity: Donate a diamond or another colorless gem, silk clothes, dairy cream, yogurt, scented oils, sugar, cow dung, or camphor to a poor young woman on Friday evening.

Fastings: On Friday, especially during Venus transits and major or minor Venus periods.

Mantra: To be chanted on Friday at sunrise, especially during major or minor Venus periods:

Shukra-astottara-shata-nama-vali
(The 108 names of *Shukra*)

Venus Astral Talisman.
Flawless diamond
handcrafted in
18k gold.
Piece no.1066

Aum shukraya namah
Aum shucaye' namah
Aum shubha-gunaya namah
Aum shubha-daya namah
Aum shubha-laksanaya namah
Aum shobhanaksaya namah
Aum shubravahaya namah
Aum shuddhasphadikabhasvaraya namah
Aum dinartiharakaya namah
Aum daitya-gurave' namah
Aum deva-abhivanditaya namah
Aum kavya-asaktaya namah
Aum kama-palaya namah
Aum kavaye' namah
Aum kalyana-dayakaya namah
Aum bhadra-murtaye' namah
Aum bhadra-gunaya namah
Aum bhargavaya namah
Aum bhakta-palanaya namah
Aum bhoga-daya namah
Aum bhuvana-adhyaksaya namah
Aum bhukti-mukti-phala-pradaya namah
Aum caru-shilaya namah
Aum caru-rupaya namah
Aum caru-candra-nibhananaya namah
Aum nidhaye' namah
Aum nikhila-shastra-jnaya namah
Aum niti-vidya-dhuram-dharaya namah
Aum sarva-laksana-sampannaya namah
Aum sarva-vaguna-varjitaya namah
Aum samana-adikanir-muktaya namah
Aum sakala-gamaparagaya namah
Aum bhrigave' namah
Aum bhoga-karaya namah
Aum bhumi-sura-palana-tat-paraya namah
Aum manasvine namah
Aum manadaya namah
Aum manyaya namah
Aum mayatitaya namah
Aum maha-yashase' namah

Aum bali-prasannaya namah
Aum abhaya-daya namah
Aum baline namah
Aum satya-parakramaya namah
Aum bhavapasha-parityagaya namah
Aum bali-bandha-vimocakaya namah
Aum ghana-shayaya namah
Aum ghana-adhyaksaya namah
Aum kambhugrivaya namah
Aum kala-dharaya namah
Aum karunya-rasa-sampurnaya namah
Aum kalyana-guna-varddhanaya namah
Aum shvetambaraya namah
Aum svetavapushe' namah
Aum catur-bhuja-samanvitaya namah
Aum akshamala-dharaya namah
Aum acintyaya namah
Aum akshinagunabha-asuraya namah
Aum nashatra-gana-samcaraya namah
Aum nayadaya namah
Aum niti-marga-daya namah
Aum barsha-pradaya namah
Aum hrishikeshaya namah
Aum klesha-nasha-karaya namah
Aum kavaye namah
Aum cintitarya-pradaya namah
Aum shanta-mataye' namah
Aum citta-samadhi-krite' namah
Aum adhi-vyadhi-haraya namah
Aum bhurivikramaya namah
Aum punya-dayakaya namah
Aum purana-purushaya namah
Aum pujyaya namah
Aum puruhuta-adi-sannutaya namah
Aum ajeyaya namah
Aum vijitarataye' namah
Aum vividha-bharanojjvalaya namah
Aum kunda-pushpa-pratikashaya namah
Aum mandahasaya namah
Aum maha-mataye' namah
Aum mukta-phala-samanabhaya namah
Aum mukti-daya namah
Aum munisannutaya namah
Aum ratna-simhasana-rudaya namah
Aum rathasthaya namah
Aum rajataprabhaya namah
Aum surya-pragdesha-samcaraya namah
Aum sura-shatru-suhride' namah
Aum kavaye' namah
Aum tula-avrishabharashishaya namah
Aum durddharaya namah
Aum dharma-palakaya namah
Aum bhagyadaya namah
Aum bhavya-caritraya namah
Aum bhavapasha-vimotrakaya namah
Aum gauda-desh-eshvaraya namah
Aum goptre namah

Venus Astral Talisman.
Flawless diamond &
herb containers
handcrafted in
18k gold.
Piece no.1059

135

Aum gunite namah
Aum guna-vibhushanaya namah
Aum jyeshtha-nakshatra-sambhutaya namah
Aum jyeshthaya namah
Aum shreshthaya namah
Aum shuci-smitaya namah
Aum apavarga-pradaya namah
Aum anantaya namah
Aum santana-phala-dayakaya namah
Aum sarva-ishvarya-pradaya namah
Aum sarva-girvanaganasannutaya namah

Shukra seed mantra:
Aum dram drim draum sah shukraya namah.

Result: The planetary deity *Shukra* is propitiated increasing riches and conjugal bliss.

Venus Astral Talisman.
Flawless diamond
handcrafted in
18k gold.
Piece no.1062

Propitiation of Saturn (Saturday)

Charity: Donate a blue sapphire or another blue to purple gemstone, iron, steel, leather, farm land, a black cow, a cooking oven with cooking utensils, a buffalo, black mustard or black sesamum seeds, to a poor man on Saturday evening.

Fasting: On Saturday during Saturn transits, and especially major or minor Saturn periods.

Mantra: To be chanted on Saturday, two hours and forty minutes before sunset, especially during major or minor Saturn periods:

Shanya-astottara-shata-nama-vali
(The 108 names of *Shani*)

Aum shanaescaraya namah
Aum shantaya namah
Aum sarvabhistapradayine namah
Aum sharanyaya namah
Aum vagenyaya namah
Aum sarveshaya namah
Aum saumyaya namah
Aum suramvandhaya namah
Aum suralokaviharine namah
Aum sukhasonapavishtaya namah
Aum sundaraya namah
Aum ghanaya namah
Aum ghanarupaya namah
Aum ghanabharanadharine namah
Aum ghanasaravilepaya namah
Aum khadyotaya namah

Saturn Astral Talisman.
Flawless blue sapphire set
in 18k gold. Piece no.945

136

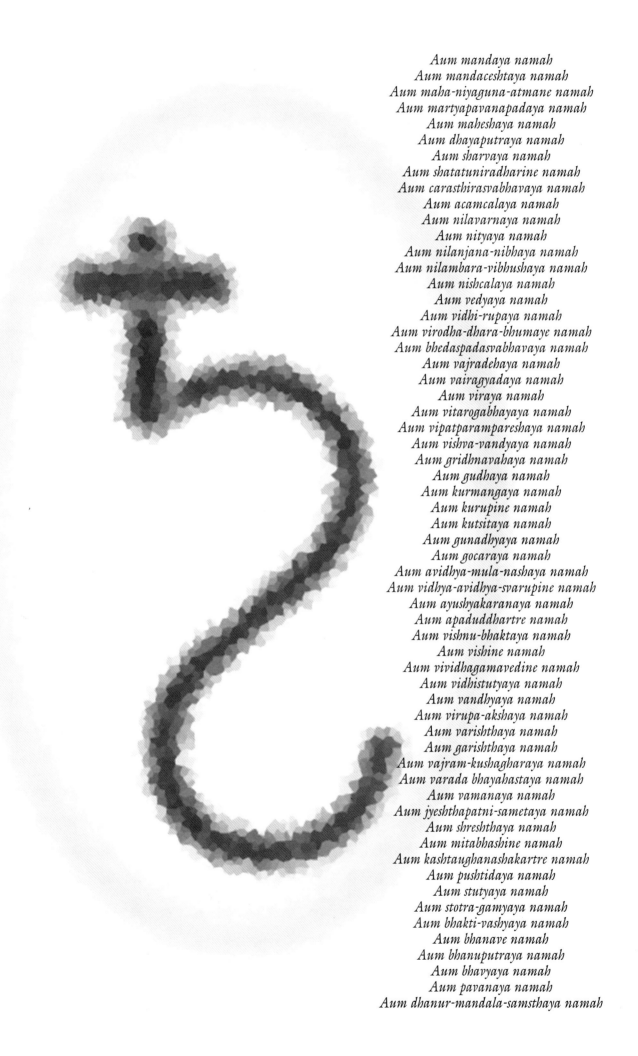

Aum mandaya namah
Aum mandaceshtaya namah
Aum maha-niyaguna-atmane namah
Aum martyapavanapadaya namah
Aum maheshaya namah
Aum dhayaputraya namah
Aum sharvaya namah
Aum shatatuniradharine namah
Aum carasthirasvabhavaya namah
Aum acamcalaya namah
Aum nilavarnaya namah
Aum nityaya namah
Aum nilanjana-nibhaya namah
Aum nilambara-vibhushaya namah
Aum nishcalaya namah
Aum vedyaya namah
Aum vidhi-rupaya namah
Aum virodha-dhara-bhumaye namah
Aum bhedaspadasvabhavaya namah
Aum vajradehaya namah
Aum vairagyadaya namah
Aum viraya namah
Aum vitarogabhayaya namah
Aum vipatparampareshaya namah
Aum vishva-vandyaya namah
Aum gridhnavahaya namah
Aum gudhaya namah
Aum kurmangaya namah
Aum kurupine namah
Aum kutsitaya namah
Aum gunadhyaya namah
Aum gocaraya namah
Aum avidhya-mula-nashaya namah
Aum vidhya-avidhya-svarupine namah
Aum ayushyakaranaya namah
Aum apaduddhartre namah
Aum vishnu-bhaktaya namah
Aum vishine namah
Aum vividhagamavedine namah
Aum vidhistutyaya namah
Aum vandhyaya namah
Aum virupa-akshaya namah
Aum varishthaya namah
Aum garishthaya namah
Aum vajram-kushagharaya namah
Aum varada bhayahastaya namah
Aum vamanaya namah
Aum jyeshthapatni-sametaya namah
Aum shreshthaya namah
Aum mitabhashine namah
Aum kashtaughanashakartre namah
Aum pushtidaya namah
Aum stutyaya namah
Aum stotra-gamyaya namah
Aum bhakti-vashyaya namah
Aum bhanave namah
Aum bhanuputraya namah
Aum bhavyaya namah
Aum pavanaya namah
Aum dhanur-mandala-samsthaya namah

Saturn Astral Talisman.
Flawless blue sapphire set
in 21k gold. Piece no.10

Aum dhanadaya namah
Aum dhanushmate namah
Aum tanu-prakasha-dehaya namah
Aum tamasaya namah
Aum asheshajanavandyaya namah
Aum visheshaphaladayine namah
Aum vashikritajaneshaya namah
Aum pashunam pataye namah
Aum khecaraya namah
Aum khageshaya namah
Aum ghana-nilambaraya namah
Aum kathinyamanasaya namah
Aum aryaganastutyaya namah
Aum nilacchatraya namah
Aum nityaya namah
Aum nirgunaya namah
Aum gunatmane namah
Aum niramayaya namah
Aum nandyaya namah
Aum vandaniyaya namah
Aum dhiraya namah
Aum divya-dehaya namah
Aum dinartiharanaya namah
Aum dainyanashakaraya namah
Aum aryajanaganyaya namah
Aum kruraya namah
Aum kruraceshtaya namah
Aum kama-krodha-karaya namah
Aum kalatraputrashatrutvakaranaya pariposhita-bhaktaya namah
Aum parabhitiharaya namah
Aum bhakta-sangha-manobhishta-phaladaya namah

Shani seed mantra: *Aum pram prim praum sah shanaisharaya namah.*

Result: The planetary deity *Shani* is pleased insuring victory in quarrels,
over coming chronic pain, and bringing success to those engaged
in the iron or steel trade.

Saturn Astral Talisman.
Flawless blue sapphire set
in 18k gold. Piece no.230

Propitiation of Rahu (Saturday)

Charity: Donate a hessonite or another fine orange gem, a coconut, old coins or coal to a leper on Saturday.

Fasting: On the first Saturday of the waxing moon, especially during major or minor *Rahu* periods.

Mantra: To be chanted on Saturday, two hours after sunset, especially during major or minor *Rahu* periods:

Rahva-astottara-shata-nama-vali
(The 108 names of *Rahu*)

Aum rahave namah
Aum saumhikeyaya namah
Aum vidhuntudaya namah
Aum surashatrave namah
Aum tamase namah
Aum phanine namah
Aum gargyaynapa namah
Aum surapye namah
Aum nibajimutasamkashaya namah
Aum caturbhujava namah
Aum khangakhetaka-dharine namah
Aum varadayakahastakaya namah
Aum shulayudhaya namah
Aum megha-varnaya namah
Aum krishna-dhvajapatakavate namah
Aum dakshinashamukharathaya namah
Aum tikshnadamshtakarallakaya namah
Aum shupokarasansthaya namah
Aum gomedha-bharana-priyaya namah
Aum mashapriyaya namah
Aum kashyaparshinandanaya namah
Aum bhujageshvaraya namah
Aum ulkapatayitre namah
Aum shuline namah
Aum nidhipaya namah
Aum krishna-sarpa-raje namah
Aum vishajvalavrita ʿasyaya addhashariraya namah
Aum shatravapradaya namah
Aum ravindubhikaraya namah
Aum chaya-svarupine namah
Aum kathinangakaya namah
Aum dvishacchatracchedakaya namah
Aum karallasyaya namah
Aum bhayamkaraya namah
Aum krura-karmane namah
Aum tamo-rupaya namah
Aum shyam-atmane namah
Aum nila-lohitaya namah
Aum kiritine namah
Aum nilavasanaya namah
Aum sanisamntavartmagaya namah
Aum candala-varnaya namah
Aum ashvyriksa-bhavaya namah
Aum mesha-bhavaya namah

Rahu Astral Talisman.
Flawless hessonite
handcrafted in 18k
gold. Piece no.673

Aum shanivat-phaladaya namah
Aum shuraya namah
Aum apasavyagataye namah
Aum uparagakagaya namah
Aum soma-surya-cchavivimardakaya namah
Aum nila-pushpa-viharaya namah
Aum graha-shreshthaya namah
Aum ashtama-grahaya namah
Aum kabamdhamatradehaya namah
Aum yatudhanakulodbhavaya namah
Aum govinda-vara-patraya namah
Aum deva-jati-pravishtakaya namah
Aum kruraya namah
Aum gharaya namah
Aum shanir-mitraya namah
Aum shukra-mitraya namah
Aum agocaraya namah
Aum mani ganga-snanadatre' namah
Aum svagrihe' pravaladhyadaya namah
Aum sad-grihe'anyabaladhrite' namah
Aum caturthe matri-nashakaya namah
Aum candrayukte candalajati sihmajanmane rajyadatre namah
Aum mahakayaya namah
Aum janma-kartre' namah
Aum vidhuripave' namah
Aum madakajnanadaya namah
Aum janmakanyarajyadatre' namah
Aum janmahanidaya namah
Aum navame pitrihantre' namah
Aum pancame' shokadayakaya namah
Aum dhyune' kalatrahantre' namah
Aum saptame kalahapradaya namah
Aum shashthe' vittadatre' namah
Aum caturthe' vairadayaka namah
Aum navame' papadatre' namah
Aum dashame shokadayakaya namah
Aum adau yashah pradatre' namah

Rahu Astral Talisman.
Flawless hessonites
handcrafted in 18k
gold. Piece no.72

140

Rahu Astral Talisman.
Flawless hessonite
handcrafted in
18k gold.
Piece no.565

Aum ante vairapradayakaya namah
Aum kalatmane' namah
Aum gocaracaraya namah
Aum ghane' kakutpradaya namah
Aum pancame' ghishanashringadaya namah
Aum svarbhanave' namah
Aum baline' namah
Aum maha-saukhya-pradayine' namah
Aum chandra-vairine namah
Aum shashvataya namah
Aum surashatrave' namah
Aum papagrahaya namah
Aum shambhavaya namah
Aum pujyakaya namah
Aum patirapuranaya namah
Aum paithinasakulodbhavaya bhakta-rakshaya namah
Aum rahu-murtaye' namah
Aum sarva-bhishta-phala-pradaya namah
Aum dirghaya namah
Aum krishnaya namah
Aum atanave' namah
Aum vishnu-netraraye' namah
Aum devaya namah
Aum danavaya namah.

Rahu seed mantra: *Aum bhram bhrim bhraum sah rahave namah.*

Result: The planetary deity *Rahu* is pleased granting victory over enemies,
favour from the King or government, and reduction
in diseases caused by *Rahu*.

Rahu & Ketu Astral
Talisman. Flawless
hessonite and cat's
eyes handcrafted
in 18k gold.
Piece no.291

Propitiation of Ketu (Thursday)

Charity: Donate a cat's eye gem, a brown cow with white spots, colored blankets, or a dog to a poor young man on Thursday.

Fasting: On the first Thursday of the waxing moon, especially during major or minor *Ketu* periods.

Mantra: To be chanted on Thursday at midnight, especially during major or minor *Ketu* periods:

Ketva-astottara-shata-nama-vali
(The 108 names of *Ketu*)

Aum ketave' namah
Aum sthulashirase' namah
Aum shiromantraya namah
Aum dhvajakrtaye' namah
Aum nava-graha-yutaya namah
Aum simhika-asuri-garbha-sambhavaya maha-bhitikaraya namah
Aum chitravarnaya namah
Aum sri-pingalaksakaya namah
Aum phulladhumasakashaya namah
Aum tishnadamshtaya namah
Aum mahodaraya namah
Aum rakta-netraya namah
Aum citra-karine namah
Aum tivrakopaya namah
Aum maha-suraya namah
Aum krura-kanthaya namah
Aum kradha-nidhaye' namah
Aum chaya-graha-vishoshakaya namah
Aum antya-grahaya namah
Aum maha-shirshaya namah
Aum surya-araye' namah
Aum pushpavad-grahine' namah
Aum varahastaya namah
Aum gadapanaye' namah
Aum citra-vastra-dharaya namah
Aum citra-dhvaja-patakaya namah
Aum ghoraya namah
Aum citra-rathaya namah
Aum shikhine' namah
Aum kullutthabhaksakaya namah
Aum vaidurya-bharanaya namah
Aum utpatajanakaya namah
Aum shukra-mitraya namah
Aum mandasakhaya namah
Aum gada-dharaya namah
Aum naka-pataye' namah
Aum antar-vedishvaraya namah
Aum jaimini-gotra-jaya namah
Aum citragupta-atmane' namah
Aum dakshina-mukhaya namah
Aum mukunda-varapatraya namah
Aum maha-asura-kulod-bhavaya namah

Ketu Astral Talisman. Flawless cat's eye handcrafted in 18k gold. Piece no.321

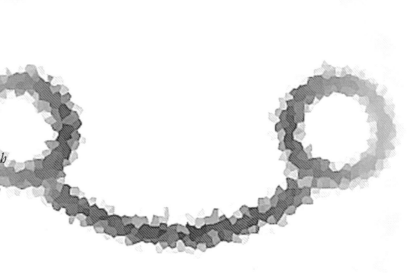

Aum ghana-varnaya namah
Aum lamba-devaya namah
Aum mrityu-putraya namah
Aum utpata-rupa-dharine' namah
Aum adrishyaya namah
Aum kala-agni-sannibhaya namah
Aum nripidaya namah
Aum griha-karine' namah
Aum sarvopadravavarakaya namah
Aum citra-prasutaya namah
Aum analaya namah
Aum sarva-vyadhi-vinashakaya namah
Aum apasavyapracarine' namah
Aum navame' papadayakaya namah
Aum pancame' shokadaya namah
Aum uparagakhe'cagaya namah
Aum ati-purushakarmane namah
Aum turiye sukhapradaya namah
Aum tritiye vairadaya namah
Aum papa-grahaya namah
Aum sphatakakarakaya namah
Aum prana-nathaya namah
Aum pancame shrimakarakaya namah
Aum dvitiye' asphutavamdatre namah
Aum vishakulitavaktakaya namah
Aum kamarupine' namah
Aum simha-dantaya namah
Aum kushedhma-priyaya namah
Aum caturthe' matrinashaya namah
Aum navame pitrenashakaya namah
Aum antye vairapradaya namah
Aum sutanandam-nidhanakaya namah
Aum sarpakshijataya namah
Aum anangaya namah
Aum karmarashyudbhavaya namah
Aum upante kirtidaya namah
Aum saptame'kalahapradaya namah
Aum ashtame' vyadhikartre' namah
Aum dhane' bahu-sukha-pradaya namah
Aum janane rogadaya namah
Aum urdhvamurdhajaya namah
Aum grahanayakaya namah
Aum papadyashtaye namah
Aum khecaraya namah
Aum shambhavaya namah
Aum asheshapujitaya namah
Aum shashvataya namah
Aum nataya namah
Aum shubhashubha-phala-pradaya namah
Aum dhumraya namah
Aum sudhapayine' namah
Aum ajitaya namah
Aum bhakta-vatsalaya namah
Aum simha-asanaya namah
Aum ketu-murtaye' namah
Aum ravindudyutinashakaya namah

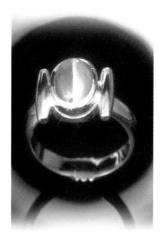

Ketu Astral Talisman.
Flawless cat's eye
handcrafted
in 18k gold.
Piece no.1040

Aum amaraya namah
Aum pidakaya namah
Aum amartya namah
Aum vishnu-drishtaya namah
Aum asureshvaraya namah
Aum bhakta-rakshaya namah
Aum vaicitryakapatasyandanaya namah
Aum vicitraphaladayine namah
Aum bhakta-bhishta-phala-pradaya namah

Ketu seed mantra: *Aum sram srim sraum sah ketave namah.*

Result: The planetary deity *Ketu* is pleased granting victory over enemies, favour from the King or government, and reduction in diseases caused by *Ketu.*

The Most Sacred Gem in the Vedas
Sri Salagrama Sila

Pictured is an exceptionally perfect and very rare *'Vamana'* *Salagrama Sila* adorned with the sacred *Chakra* of Lord *Visnu.* Origin: The Krsna-Gandaki river in Nepal. According to the *Gautamiya Tantra* a stone from any place other than the Gandaki River in Nepal can never be a *Salagram Sila.* Merely by touching a genuine *Salagrama Sila* one is relieved of the sins of millions of births, so what to speak of worshipping Him. By *puja* of *Salagrama Sila* one gains the direct association of Lord *Hari.* The *Skanda Purana* states that a genuine *Salagrama Sila* is directly a manifestation of the Supreme Lord *Visnu* and does not require any installation. It is further stated that the sale or purchase of a *Salagrama Sila* is strictly prohibited. Anyone who attempts to determine the material value of a *Salagrama Sila* will live in hell until the end of the universe. The area within a radius of 24 miles from where a *Salagrama Sila* is worshipped is considered a holy place *(tirtha).* Anyone who sees, bathes, worships, or bows to a *Salagrama Sila* will receive the same piety as doing millions of sacrifices and giving millions of cows in charity.

Without having accumulated pious activities, it is very difficult to find a *Salagrama Sila* in this world, especially in the age of *Kali-yuga.* In the *Padma Purana* it is stated, were a devotee properly initiated in prescribed mantras do the *puja* of *Salagrama Sila* he will attain the Supreme Lord's spiritual abode without a doubt.

Servitor: *Hrisikesananda dasa*
Photo: Adisorn Wattanavanich
Sastric evidence: *Sri Hari-bhakti-vilas, translated by Sri Padmanabha Goswami, Sri Radha-ramana Temple,* Vrndavana, U.P., India

Glossary

ADULARESCENCE : An optical phenomenon applied to orthoclase or adulria feldspar that exhibits a floating, billowy, white or bluish light effect.

AGGREGATE : Crystalline aggregate made up of many particles, each an individual crystal too small to be seen by the unaided eye.

BIREFRINGENCE : The strength of double refraction measured by taking the difference between the high and low refractive indices of a doubly refractive gemstone.

CRYSTAL SYSTEM : One of the six groups of crystal patterns in which minerals and other crystalline solids occur. They are : cubic, tetragonal, hexagonal, orthorhombic, monoclinic and triclinic.

CUBIC : Highly symmetrical crystal system with three equal crystallographic axes at right angles.

DICHROISM : The property of doubly refractive colored gemstones of transmitting two different colors in two different directions caused by their unequal absorption of the two portions of a doubly refracted beam of light.

DISPERSION : The property of a transparent gemstone to separate white light into its component colors.

DOUBLE REFRACTION : The property of separating a single ray of light into two.

FLUORESCENCE : The emission of visible light by a gem when exposed to ultra-violet or X-radiation.

HEXAGONAL : A crystal system having three equal axes at 60 degrees and a fourth axes perpendicular to the other three and unequal in length.

INCLUSION : Any internal foreign body or imperfection in a gem.

MANTRAM : A combination of transcendental sound vibrations with the power to deliver the mind from material limitations and invoke a higher state of being.

MATRIX : The rock in which a mineral is contained.

MOHS SCALE : The most commonly used scale of relative hardness of minerals with numbers from one to ten assigned to ten minerals of increasing hardness from talc to diamond.

MONOCLINIC :	A crystal system with two axes unequal in length at right angles to one another and a third axes of unequal length which is not at right angles to the plane of the other two.
OPTIC CHARACTER:	The nature of a gem as either uniaxial (singly refractive) or biaxial (doubly refractive.)
ORIENT:	The iridescent luster of a pearl.
ORTHORHOMBIC:	A crystal system with three axes of unequal length, each perpendicular to the plane of the other two axes.
PLEOCHROISM:	The property of most doubly refractive colored gemstones of exhibiting either two or more different colors when observed through a dichroscope in transmitted light.
REFRACTIVE INDEX:	A measure of the amount a light ray is bent as it enters or leaves a gemstone.
SIDEREAL:	Pertaining to the stars. Time as measured by the apparent motion of the constellations and planets.
SINGLE REFRACTION:	When a light ray enters either an isometric or amorphous gem substance, it remains intact and is refracted in the normal manner as a singly ray.
SPECIFIC GRAVITY:	The ratio of the weight of a gemstone to that of an equal volume of water at 4°c.
STOTRAM:	A prayer and invocation.
TETRAGONAL:	A crystal system with two axes equal in length and at right angles with a third axes at right angles to the first two.
TRICHROISM:	The property of most doubly refractive, colored gemstones belonging to the orthorhombic, monoclinic, and triclinic crystal systems, of transmitting three different colors in three different directions when observed through a dichroscope in transmitted light.
TRICLINIC:	The least symmetrical crystal system with three axes, no two of which are of equal length and no two of which are perpendicular to one another.

Bibliography

M.N. Dutt (translator). *Garuda Puranam.* The Chowkhamba Sanskrit Series Office, Varanasi-1, India. 1968.

M.N. Dutt (translator). *Agni Puranam.* The Chowkhamba Sanskrit Series Office, Varanasi-1, India. 1967.

Radhakrishna Parasara. *Ratna-vijnana.* The Chowkhamba Vidyabhawan, Varanasi, U.P., India. 1972.

A. K. Bhattacharya. *Gem Therapy.* Firma KLM Pvt. Ltd., 257- B.B. Ganguly Street, Calcutta - 12. India. 1971.

P. N. Scherman. *Gems and Their Occult Powers.* Scherman, 68/6 Kidwai Nagar, Ext. - 1, Kanpur, India. 1979.

N. N. Saha. *Precious Stones That Heal.* Allied Publishers Pvt., Ltd., 13/14 Asaf Ali Road, New Delhi 110002, India. 1980.

Raj Roop Tank. *Indian Gemology.* Dulichand Kirtichand Tank, Johari Bazaar, Jaipur 302003, India. 1971.

Dr. G. S. Kapur. *Ratna-pradip.* Goyal & Co., Dariba, Delhi-110006, India. 1974.

Dr. Narayana Dutt Srimali. *Jyotish & Ratna.* Kusum Prakasan, 17 Shivacharan Lal Road, Ilahabad-3, India. 1975.

Richard T. Liddicoat, Jr. *Handbook of Gem Identification.* G.I.A., 1660 Stewart Street, Santa Monica, Calif. 90406, U.S.A. 1981.

Tom Hopke. *How to Read Your Horoscope.* The Vedic Cultural Assn., 51 Coelho Way, Honolulu, Hawaii 95817, U.S.A. 1988.

Richard S. Brown. *Handbook of Planetary Gemology.* Mckinney Intl., P.O. Box 98842, T.S.T., Hong Kong. 1988.

G. F. Kunz. *The Curious Lore of Precious Stones.* Dover Publications, Inc., 180 Varick St., New York 10014. 1971.

S. M. Tagore. *Mani-Mala.* I. C. Bose & Co., Calcutta, India. 1879.

Prof. B. V. Raman. *Astrology For Beginners.* IBH Prakashana, Fifth Main, Gandhinagar, Bangalore-560 009, India. 1983.

A.T. Mann. *The Round Art.* Dragon's World Ltd. 1979

Dr. G. S. Kapoor. *Gems and Astrology.* Ranjan Publications, 16 Ansari Road, Daryaganj, New Delhi-110002, India. 1991.

Dr. G. S. Kapoor. *Remedial Measures In Astrology.* Ranjan Publications, 16 Ansari Road, Daryaganj, New Delhi-110002, India. 1990.

J. N. Bhasin. *Dictionary of Astrology.* Ranjan Publications, 16 Ansari Road, Daryaganj, New Delhi-110002, India. 1988.

About the Author

Richard S. Brown (*Hrisikesananda dasa*) enjoyed his first taste of fame as the lead singer of the innovative rock group 'The Missunderstood', which rose to stardom in London during the late sixties. Later he became a disciple of the great Indian Guru *Swami Bhaktivedanta* and subsequently moved to India to study religion at the holy pilgrimage town of *Vrindaban*. For seven years he lived the strictly ascetic life of a traditional monk and devoteed himself entirely to religious practice and public service. During this time he helped build two schools, lectured extensively on religion throughout India, became proficient in *Sanskrit* and was befriended by the President, Chief Justice, and other prominent Indian dignitaries.

Eventually he became involved in a secret ruby mine located in Southern India. This experience sparked his interest in gems and inspired him to undertake an in-depth study of the ancient *Sanskrit* classics dealing with gemology. Combining technical knowledge of gems with the planetary aspects revealed in the ancient texts, Richard Brown began to develop his own unique system of designing auspicious Astral Gemstone Talismans. In 1979, after 12 years in Asia, he returned to America to complete his formal training at the Gemological Institute of America (G.I.A.). Thereafter he returned to Thailand, where he has firmly established himself as an international authority on gemstones and a renowned designer of Astral Gemstone Talisman jewelry.

Richard Brown is also the author of several books on astral gemstones and their powers, including the **Handbook of Planetary Gemology** and **Ancient Astrological Gemstones and Talismans.** He has lectured extensively throughout the world on topics of 'Planetary Gemology' at conventions and seminars sponsored by gemological as well as by metaphysical and occult associations. A book based on his life was written in 1988 by the Asia-based American writer Daniel P. Reid.

Ketu Astral Talisman. Flawless cat's eye & herb container handcrafted in 21k gold. Piece no.854